# HION

## A Rational Guide for Understanding Acid-Base Relationships of Normal and Clinical Phenomena

S. Richard Heisey, Sc.D.

Thomas Adams, Ph.D.

*Michigan State University*
*Department of Physiology*

The McGraw-Hill Companies, Inc.

Boston  Burr Ridge, IL  Dubuque, IA  Madison, WI  New York  San Francisco
St. Louis  Bangkok  Bogotá  Caracas  Lisbon  London  Madrid  Mexico City  Milan
New Delhi  Paris  Seoul  Singapore  Sydney  Taipei  Toronto

*McGraw-Hill Higher Education*
*A Division of The McGraw-Hill Companies*

HION

A Rational Guide for Understanding Acid-Base Relationships of Normal and Clinical Phenomena

1 2 3 4 5 6 7 8 9 0   QSR  QSR   0 9 8 7 6 5 4 3 2

ISBN 0-07-285312-3

Editor: Lynn Nordbrock
Production Editor: Lynn Nagel
Cover Design: Sylvester Bal-Bio
Printer/Binder: Quebecor World

# Table of Contents

# Preface

This book comes from decades of teaching physiological principles to advanced undergraduates, graduate students and medical students. This experience shows there are polar educational forces at work when it comes to presenting acid-base phenomena. On one side, it's temptingly expedient to describe very simple analyses and uncomplicated equations using very few variables. Most textbooks do this. The attraction for both instructors and students, of course, is that just a couple of hours is all that's required to get a working knowledge about how pH is controlled in body fluids. Never mind it is fragmentary and in some parts wrong. At a superficial level, though, it sure looks easy to become an acid-base expert. Many people consider they are.

On the other side, the physical chemical and physiological phenomena which control hydrogen ion concentration in body fluids are extremely complex and difficult to understand, even for those who work in the area. Just scratching the surface of the simple explanations, though, soon shows there is much greater depth of information and analysis to explore and far greater understanding to gain. But, where do you find a balance between the overly simplistic and the inappropriately detailed extremes?

Settling out-of-hand for just the simplest explanation gives poor service. Not only is it intellectually offensive, it also leaves too many questions unanswered. Superficial analyses present such a fragile and unstable base for understanding acid-base phenomena that speculation, unsubstantiated theories, and imagined membrane phenomena must be concocted to shore up the arguments. Almost without exception, they are unsuccessful in bridging the span between best-guesses and measured reality. The clinical phenomenon of the "anion gap", for example, bears witness that there are ionic and osmotic forces afoot, which are not evaluated in only Henderson- Hasselbalch calculations and in the minimally good-enough explanations given most medical students. There would be no "gap" in ionic accountability were more of the pertinent variables measured and their effects considered.

This book is written for those who are dissatisfied with the just good-enough analyses for examining acid-base status. The information it contains, though, is not new. The physical chemical and biochemical fundamentals it quotes have been known for years. Why, then, has a book like this one not appeared before? There are several reasons, most of which bear on the unavoidably reductionist quality of information in the basic sciences.

It's hard to bring together for easy reading important details of biochemistry, physiology, physical chemistry, membrane phenomena and clinical medicine. Even if this information were presented clearly and succinctly in the scientific literature in each field, when, in fact, much of it is not, there are still a lot of facts to be evaluated, equations to be reviewed and theories to be reconciled. Not an easy task. This book attempts to compile the more pertinent concepts found only in the original scientific literature into an easily read, accurate and internally consistent story of how the body's hydrogen ion concentration is established. It is more a translation and interpretation of the existing scientific literature than it is a contribution to it.

Doing justice to all the appropriate fundamentals does not, however, always make for smooth going. The book is organized to help with this by presenting in Chapter 1 generally well known phenomena about the acid-base status of major body fluids. It also provides basic information about how hydrogen ion concentration is measured and numerically expressed. Chapter 2 describes principles for how molecules and ions exist in equilibria in aqueous solutions and introduces pivotal concepts about the electrical neutrality of water. This chapter also describes important relationships associated with a solution's strong ion difference.

Using the principles presented in Chapters 1 and 2, Chapter 3 shows how dissolved carbon dioxide in inanimate and in biological fluids operates as an independent force for establishing a protein-free solution's hydrogen ion concentration. Chapter 4 defines the additional effects of non-volatile weak acids in establishing pH for plasma and intracellular fluid and describes the role of proteins and inorganic phosphate in biological fluids. This chapter closes by introducing a new mathematical model for expressing acid-base relationships and describing the roles of albumin and inorganic phosphate.

Chapter 5 highlights how interstitial and intracellular fluids, along with blood plasma, strike a balance among the many forces operating on them to remain within normal ranges of pH. This chapter also shows how highly acidic gastric juice is formed and how pancreatic juice becomes so strongly alkaline. Comparisons are made between standard explanations for these phenomena and how the principles in this book are relevant for providing simpler and more rational explanations for these phenomena. Chapter 6 reviews the pathophysiology of acid-base status. It describes commonly used diagnostic strategies for respiratory and non-respiratory (a.k.a. metabolic) challenges to acid-base status and explains how compensatory mechanisms usually reestablish pH to be in a normal range.

We suggest this book can be read at several levels. Just reviewing its main physiological, biochemical and clinical information gives a much more detailed, integrated and useful basis for understanding acid-base status, than does reading any contemporary textbook. There is still more information, though, for those who need to examine the derivation of each equation and look more closely at it all. We hope there is something here not only for every student in the basic sciences, but also for practicing professionals, especially physicians.

# Introduction

Listen to conversation about acid-base balance going on in any group of biologists, physiologists, pharmacologists, biochemists, zoologists, physicians, or others who have been professionally trained in recent years. Prospects are that within no more than a few minutes you'll start hearing references to the Henderson-Hasselbalch equation and learn about the information it purports to convey. Chances are also you'll soon get wind of incorrect statements based on common misconceptions and misinterpretations of its relationships. It's unavoidable.

Paying close attention, it's likely you will hear, for example, about how the ratio of bicarbonate ions to dissolved carbon dioxide in a body fluid determines its pH. **Not true.** You might also discover that the hydrogen ion concentration of a body fluid depends on how much bicarbonate ion is either retained, or removed by the kidney. **Not true.** If you listen carefully and long enough, you'll also learn that acid-base status is quickly and easily changed by "injecting, or administering bicarbonate". **Not true.** No doubt you will see heads nod in the group when someone refers to how much hydrochloric acid is secreted by the stomach. **Not true.** Neither the stomach, nor any other body organ secretes it.

No doubt you will overhear that bicarbonate and chloride ions are counter transported at cell membranes. **Not true.** You might even learn that, "Our direct measurements of bicarbonate ion show that. . ." **Not true** - such a measurement is impossible. No one in the group is likely to challenge the statement that, "The Henderson-Hasselbalch equation shows how much acid or base there is in a body fluid". **Not true.** The equation is fundamentally accurate and of considerable value, but this is not what it reports.

So much for eavesdropping on people who've been traditionally trained, some of whom might even be authors of popular and widely quoted contemporary textbooks. Were you to confront these people making such erroneous statements, the counter might be, "But the Henderson-Hasselbalch equation shows that . . ." **No it doesn't.** It doesn't support any of these myths.

Are, then, relationships expressed in the Henderson-Hasselbalch equation incorrect? No, they're not. But, their interpretations may very well be, especially when inferences are drawn by those who do not understand how the equation was originally derived and what it was intended to imply. As for many ethical and religious statements, there's nothing wrong with the statement itself - the devil lies in the interpretation.

The major goal of this book is to ask readers to reexamine the premises for the Henderson-Hasselbalch equation, and for many other similar relationships, in the light of the physical chemical and biological phenomena on which they are based. This is not an easy task. The reader must not only remain inquisitive and open-minded, but also be willing to consider details about biological fluids and their dissolved ions and molecules, which are all too often overlooked in most textbooks.

Although the journey through information in this book will be necessarily complex, its starting point is very simple and intuitive. No one doubts that an aqueous solution is electrically neutral, simply because it contains the same concentrations of anions and cations. Put two electrodes in any cell, body fluid or body compartment, or in just a glass of plain water, for that matter, to discover there is not a voltage difference anywhere within the fluid, no matter what its composition. Sprinkle table salt in the glass of water to find there still isn't a voltage gradient anywhere in it. Add a teaspoon of bicarbonate of soda, vinegar, or anything else, stir it up and its voltage still doesn't change. Similarly for any living cell, there certainly may be voltage gradients across a cell membrane, but not in the solutions on either side of the membrane. All insight about acid-base phenomena described in this book rests solely on the simple, uncontested, incontrovertible and easily-tested principle that an aqueous solution contains equal concentrations of positive and negative charges. We'll let the reader take it step-by-step from there, starting at Chapter 1.

There are two basic concepts on which to depend when reading this book. One is that an aqueous solution does not have a voltage gradient anywhere in it. The other is that there are obligatory cause-and-effect relationships between and among materials in a solution. Some function as independent variables and others respond to them as dependent variables. For example, a solution's hydrogen, hydroxyl, bicarbonate and carbonate ion concentrations (dependent variables) depend on its concentrations of independent variables carbon dioxide, protein, inorganic phosphate and the difference between the concentrations of strong cations and strong anions. Diet, exercise, respiration, renal function, among other metabolic phenomena, establish these independent variables, which drive the solution's acid-base status through effects on its dependent variables.

In this context, an independent variable is any factor imposed on an aqueous solution, which obligates changes in its composition of dependent variables to retain electrical neutrality. Blood plasma, cerebrospinal fluid, interstitial fluid and intracellular fluid are each separate fluid compartments, whose concentrations of hydrogen, bicarbonate, hydroxyl and carbonate ions (dependent variables) respond to effects imposed by independent variables from outside the solution, for example, carbon dioxide, weak non-volatile acids and non-reacting strong ions.

The reward for reading this book is that it will dispel mysteries about how acid-base status is achieved in every fluid compartment in the body, no matter where and for what species. It will also be revealed how pH can be so low in some body fluids, as in gastric juice, yet so high in others, as in pancreatic juice. Look also for information about how the pH at the upper end of the gastrointestinal tract can be as low as it ever gets through a biological process, but can be as high as it ever gets at the lower end of the gut, just a short distance away in the same contiguous tube. The book will also reveal the thermodynamic and physical chemical bases which govern the fluid compartment hydrogen ion concentration in every known life form, from unicellular organisms to humans.

Without being contentious, this book is by its very nature iconoclastic. It brings under the bright light of detailed analysis many of the "everyone knows that" statements about acid-base status and about how each body fluid is unique in establishing its own aqueous, molecular and ionic composition. Open any contemporary textbook to read broadly stated, unsupported, sometimes fanciful, and incorrect conclusions about acid-base status, not only in the basic biological sciences, but in clinical medicine, too. How ironic and potentially damaging, if not just intellectually inadequate, it is that the mechanisms for one of the body's pervasive, most important and significant life-supporting functions, the regulation of acid-base status, are so commonly misrepresented and so often stated overly simplistically. The reader is invited to challenge them with the information presented in this book. It'll be worth it.

# Chapter 1

## Acid-Base Relationships to Body Fluids

**What to Look for:**

In this chapter you will learn about:

- the importance of acid-base balance in biological processes
- how the pH scale is constructed and how it's used
- relationships between a fluid's hydrogen ion concentration and its pH
- the importance of water in biological systems
- fluid compartments of the body
- ionic concentrations in different body fluids
- how cell membrane permeability, diffusion and metabolic processes affect the distribution of materials in the body
- how molecules and ions in body fluids affect pH

All animals regulate acid-base status by indirectly affecting the concentration of hydrogen ions in their body fluids. The need for such maintenance is that hydrogen ion concentration is a pivotal factor in setting the rate and direction of chemical reactions on which depend digestion, metabolism, cell repair, nerve function, body movements, enzyme activity, and most other life processes. In most body fluids, hydrogen ion concentration is much lower than that of other ions - in gastric juice, it is adjusted to be very high.

This manuscript describes operations of the two major mechanisms by which hydrogen ion concentration is regulated in mammals, including humans. One is through the physical chemical relationships between cations and anions contained in body fluids. Renal and gastrointestinal functions are the primary processes that slowly set body hydration and electrolyte concentrations for this to happen. The other is through the rapid control of carbon dioxide partial pressure in blood and other body fluids, for which respiratory functions provide the primary regulation. Renal and respiratory processes working together continually control hydrogen ion concentration to be within narrow limits, even in the face of metabolic, dietary and exercise loads.

Many factors determine acid-base status. The ideas that underlie their complex interactions are not only difficult for many to understand, they are also challenging to apply accurately. This book is a step-by-step introduction to these thermodynamic and physiological events and describes

> Many life processes depend on hydrogen ion concentration in different body fluids set through respiratory, metabolic and renal functions.

the importance of acid-base status in many biological processes. It emphasizes that a body fluid's hydrogen ion concentration depends only on dissolved carbon dioxide and on the concentration and valence of other ions in the solution. Understanding these relationships is important for accurately interpreting pH and seeing its biological significance.

This chapter first introduces the pH scale and the relationships between hydrogen ion concentration and pH. It then describes basic phenomena associated with water, defines the body's fluid compartments, describes their ionic composition and shows the importance of cell membrane characteristics, diffusion and metabolic processes in establishing them. Next, it shows how strong ions and carbon dioxide affect a solution's hydrogen ion concentration, thereby setting its acid-base status. Examples are given throughout the book not only for inanimate aqueous solutions, but also for intracellular and extracellular body fluid compartments.

# Section A

## The pH Scale - One Way to Describe Acid-Base Relationships

Hydrogen ion concentration is normally diminishingly small in comparison with other electrically active materials dissolved in body fluids (Table 1-2). Sodium ions, for example, are about 3.5 million times more concentrated and $HCO_3^-$ about 600,000 times more concentrated in blood plasma than are $H^+$'s. $H^+$, however, is nonetheless essential in life processes. Despite its only single positive charge, it carries a dense electrical field gradient. Hydrogen ion strongly influences reactions among other molecules in its environment. It determines, for example, the structure and configurational strength of proteins. Also, it is involved in the processes of binding $O_2$ to hemoglobin and it is essential in many other biochemical reactions, as well as being a byproduct of many reactions.

The importance of $H^+$ in life processes has been recognized for a long time. Many strategies and nomenclatures have been promoted in the past century to express its concentration, symbolized as "$[H^+]$". A challenge to all is that there is a large range of $[H^+]$ in aqueous solutions, but that compatible with life is relatively

> Although the body's hydrogen ion concentration is small, it has a powerful influence on protein configuration, hemoglobin binding with oxygen and on many other functions.

small. The problem has been to devise a scale for expressing [H$^+$] using a convenient and simple numerical statement. Although it is accurate, it would be awkward to indicate, for example, that [H$^+$] in a solution decreased from 0.0000000398 Eq/L to one of 0.0000000316 Eq/L. A simpler and more easily read expression would be useful.

One answer to the problem of expressing [H$^+$] was introduced about a century ago (Astrup & Severinghaus, 1986; Cohen & Kassirer, 1982) with the so-called "pH" scale, symbolizing the power ("Pouvoir") of hydrogen ("Hydrogène"). The pH of a solution is calculated as the logarithm of the reciprocal of [H$^+$] in units of Eq/L , that is: pH $= \log_{10}(1/[\text{H}^+])$. For example, a solution with a [H$^+$] of 0.0000000398 Eq/L is expressed as having a pH of 7.4, that is:

$$pH = \log_{10}(1/3.98 \times 10^{-8}) = \log_{10}(25,125,628.14) = 7.4$$

Similarly, one with a pH of 7.5 would have a [H$^+$] of 0.0000000316 Eq/L. The pH scale is useful to chemists, physical chemists, chemical engineers, as well as to physiologists, biochemists and others as a dimensionless expression (it has no units itself) using a simple number format to report non-linearly [H$^+$]. Data in Figure 1-1 and Table 1-1 show relationships between pH and [H$^+$] over a small range.

Despite its general usefulness and widespread acceptance in scientific and medical circles, accurate and appropriate interpretations of the pH

> Small increases in pH represent non-linear decreases in [H$^+$] and *vice versa*.

scale require some insight. For example, although a pH value is a dimensionless number, its calculation must be made on the basis of [H$^+$] in units of Eq/L. It is

| Table 1-1: pH and [H$^+$] Relationships | | | |
|---|---|---|---|
| pH | [H$^+$] (Eq/L) | [H$^+$] (Eq/L) | [H$^+$] (nEq/L) |
| 7.0 | 1 x 10$^{-7}$ | 0.0000001 | 100 |
| 7.2 | 6.31 x 10$^{-8}$ | 0.0000000631 | 63.1 |
| 7.4 | 3.98 x 10$^{-8}$ | 0.0000000398 | 39.8 |
| 7.6 | 2.51 x 10$^{-8}$ | 0.0000000251 | 25.1 |
| 7.8 | 1.58 x 10$^{-8}$ | 0.0000000158 | 15.8 |
| 8.0 | 1 x 10$^{-8}$ | 0.00000001 | 10 |

important to recognize that a numerical increase in a pH number represents a non-linear decrease in [H$^+$] and consequently a decrease in acidity, and *vice versa*.

Remembering how pH is calculated for a solution is important for seeing how its change relates to a corresponding change in [H$^+$]. As shown in Figure 1-1 and Table 1-1, small changes in pH represent disproportionately large changes in [H$^+$], which is a mathematical consequence of how pH is calculated. For example, grapefruit has a pH of about 3.1. The juice of a lemon has a pH of about 2.3, only 0.8 pH unit below that of grapefruit. Yet, there is over a 530% increase in [H$^+$] for the more acid solution. Also, a non-

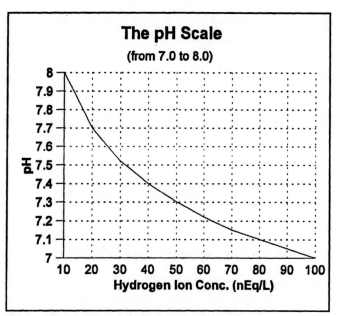

Figure 1-1: pH decreases non-linearly as a function of increasing hydrogen ion concentration.

respiratory (so-called "metabolic") acidosis, for example, as the result of an
inadequately treated and uncompensated diabetes mellitus may reduce plasma pH from a normal value of 7.4, to one of 7.1. Although this is only a decrease of a 0.3 pH unit, it represents a doubling of $[H^+]$. A

> The pH scale, like the Richter Scale for earthquake intensity, is non-linear. Small changes in values on these scales represent much larger increments in the phenomena they index.

similar increase in acidity might arise because of a chronic obstructive respiratory disease, like emphysema or chronic bronchitis, that induces hypoventilation and a retention of $CO_2$. These changes in $[H^+]$ have powerful biological consequences.

Although the pH scale accurately represents the $[H^+]$ in a solution, it by no means reveals all the biological factors that contribute to acid-base status. $[H^+]$ is the net result of many direct and indirect, simultaneously interacting metabolic, biochemical and physiological processes.

# Section B

## Volume, Location and Composition of Body Fluid Compartments

### B.1. Water in Biological Systems

All known life processes depend on water and on the materials dissolved in it. Water is not only the most common molecule on the surface of the earth, it is also the most abundant in the human body (for an adult, about 42 Liters) and most highly concentrated (55.5 mol/L), accounting for about 60% of its total weight. It is important not only as the body's "universal solvent" in which all other materials are dissolved, but it is also a source of $H^+$ and $OH^-$ when it dissociates to play an important role in acid-base status.

Body water constantly exists in two forms, as it does in simple aqueous solutions. It occurs as an electrically neutral molecule ($H_2O$) and as its dissociated ions, $H^+$ and $OH^-$. When body temperature increases, more molecular water converts to dissociated ions, and *vice versa.* The

> Water is the most abundant molecule in the body. Although it is primarily an undissociated molecule, it also plays an important role in setting pH by contributing $H^+$ and $OH^-$.

rate of dissociation is expressed in the equilibrium (or dissociation) constant ($K_w$) for water, which is low at temperatures compatible with life. At 37°C, for example, it is only $4.33 \times 10^{-16}$ Eq/L (Harned & Owen, 1958). This means that water in living systems normally exists predominantly as the undissociated, uncharged molecule, $H_2O$. The consequence is that small increases in temperature do not substantially decrease the concentration of water as an electrically neutral, undissociated molecule, even though the additional heat promotes higher circulating concentrations of $H^+$ and $OH^-$. Water in living systems serves not only as the principle diluent, but also as a source of cations and anions.

All life processes are dynamic - they constantly change. None is static. But, some change faster than others. Soft tissue and bone masses and their composition, for example, change much more slowly (typically over months and years) than do body temperature and body water

> No life processes are equilibria, which are balances between, or among, static phenomena. All are steady states, which are balances between, or among, dynamic and constantly changing phenomena.

(typically over minutes and hours). For all, however, a stable status (steady state) at any moment is a function of the balance between net rates of gain and net rates of loss. There are such steady states not only for masses and volumes in the body, like water and the materials dissolved in it, but also for its energy content, like heat.

The concentration and amount of water in the body at any time is a balance between the net rates at which this molecule is gained and those at which it is lost. For most animals, water is gained by the periodic ingestion of both liquids and solid foods that contain water. It is also produced as a byproduct of metabolism. Body water is lost primarily by urination and defecation and as an invisible vapor in expired air. It is lost to a substantially lesser extent by the formation of tears, expelled saliva and by diffusion as invisible water vapor through the skin. There may be much higher rates of water loss, however, in humans by sweating, approaching rates as high as 4 L/hr. In contrast, some animals reduce water losses so effectively, that water in their solid food and that produced just by metabolism is enough to keep them adequately hydrated. They never drink liquid water.

## B.2. Body Fluid Compartments

Regardless of the effectiveness of body water conservation, all animals, including humans, must not only keep total body water within a narrow range, it must also be precisely distributed among different body compartments (Figure 1-2). Because there are no cellular or compartmental barriers to the movement of water in the body, it diffuses freely and passively along osmotic concentration gradients.

The largest volume of body water (up to 60% of the total) is inside cells. The remainder (extracellular fluid) is between cells (interstitial fluid), in plasma and inside red blood cells, with a small amount ("other fluids") sequestered as cerebrospinal and synovial fluids, gastric and pancreatic juices, the aqueous humor of the eye, saliva and as other, small volumes.

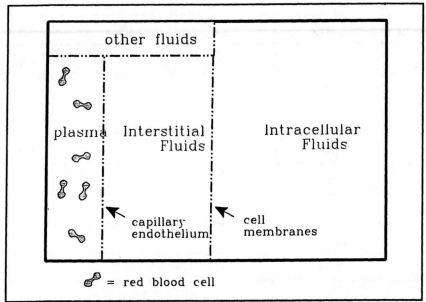

**Figure 1-2:** Body Fluid Compartments. Total body fluid (42 L) is distributed among intracellular (23 L) and interstitial (13.5 L) compartments and in plasma (3 L), red blood cells (2 L) and other fluids (0.5 L) like cerebrospinal fluid, gastric and pancreatic juices, aqueous humor of the eye, etc. Extracellular fluid = interstitial fluid + blood plasma + other fluids.

All parts of the body share whatever water it contains. Different body compartments, however, typically control their molecular and ionic composition. This gives rise to great regional differences in acidity, but not in osmolarity, except regionally at microscopic levels. Though the skin of all animals is an essential barrier to water

Water freely diffuses throughout the body. Even so, all animals closely regulate the volume of water and the concentration of dissolved materials in each of their body fluid compartments.

exchanges with their environments, water readily diffuses among body tissues. Ionic concentrations for body fluid compartments are shown in Table 1-2.

| Table 1-2: Ion Concentrations in Body Fluids (Stewart, 1981) | | | | |
|---|---|---|---|---|
| *Ion* | *Intracellular* | *Interstitial* | *Plasma* | *Red Blood Cell* |
| $Na^+$ (mEq/L) | 10 | 137 | 143 | 19 |
| $K^+$ (mEq/L) | 155 | 3 | 4 | 95 |
| $Mg^{2+}$ (mEq/L) | 10 | 2 | 2 | 5 |
| $Ca^{2+}$ (mEq/L) | undefined | 1 | 1 | undefined |
| $Cl^-$ (mEq/L) | 10 | 111 | 107 | 52 |
| other* | 35 | 1 | 1 | 10 |
| $HCO_3^-$ (mEq/L) | 12 | 31 | 25 | 15 |
| $OH^-$ (µEq/L) | 0.4 | 1.1 | 1.1 | 0.7 |
| $H^+$ (nEq/L) | 100 | 41 | 40 | 64 |

* strong anions (sulphate$^{2-}$, lactate$^-$, etc.)

## B.3. The Importance of Membrane Permeability, Diffusion and Metabolic Processes

Water, dissolved carbon dioxide and oxygen, and electrically neutral, small molecules move freely and rapidly throughout the body along concentration gradients. The differences in volume and ionic composition of body fluid compartments

> All body fluid compartments are electrically neutral.

come only from a few factors. They depend on the permeability characteristics of cell membranes and capillary endothelia, the electromotive forces (voltages) maintained across them, and metabolic forces moving molecules (so-called "active transport"). These are powerful influences, in addition to particle size and concentration gradient, that define how electrically charged particles (ions, molecules and proteins) and electrically neutral, large molecules are concentrated in body fluid compartments.

Membrane permeability alone is an important factor in distributing molecules among body fluid compartments. For example, the endothelial membrane lining all capillaries separates the interstitial fluid surrounding organ cells and tissues from perfusing blood. It is permeable to water and dissolved gases, of course, but also allows passage of ions and selective large molecules by bulk filtration and reabsorption along concentration gradients. This is how gases, nutrients and metabolic waste products are exchanged. The endothelial membrane, however, is substantially less permeable to large proteins in plasma, so virtually none normally appears in interstitial fluid. Similarly, red blood cells are essential for the body's transport of oxygen and carbon dioxide because their membranes are freely permeable to dissolved gases, but impermeable to their contained hemoglobin molecules.

The ionic and molecular composition of most fluid compartments depends on the net effects of membrane permeability, metabolically-driven active transport, transmembrane voltage and chemical concentration gradients. For example,

> Each body fluid compartment is self-regulated to have a unique composition, osmolarity , and pH.

cerebrospinal fluid surrounding the brain and spinal cord has a unique composition because of its formation in the choroid plexuses by both passive diffusion and active transport mechanisms. Similarly, the intracellular fluid of all nerve cells depends on the gated control of ionic flux across cell membranes along electrical and chemical concentration gradients, as well as by the distribution of ions by active transport.

# Section C

## Aqueous Solutions and Their Dissolved Ions

Understanding the mechanisms of acid-base balance in living systems depends on knowing something about the properties of aqueous solutions. Pure water exists only in the laboratory in the form of distilled water. More commonly, volumes of water, either in the natural world or as parts of living systems, contain many different dissolved molecules and ions.

An ion is any material in a water solution that carries an electrical charge. Some combine with other ions to form uncharged molecules. Others remain free in the solution as electrically charged particles. There are similarities between the ionic composition of water solutions outside the body and those in all living systems, like plants, microorganisms and larger animals, including humans. Ions are characterized by their polarity and strength of electrical charge.

> Ions are characterized by their polarity and the strength of their electrical charge (valence).

Cations, for example, carry one or more positive charges; anions carry one or more negative charges. Ions are often elemental particles, like $H^+$, $K^+$, $Ca^{2+}$, or $Cl^-$, but also may be complex molecules, like $SO_4^{2-}$, $PO_4^{3-}$, carboxyl ($COO^-$) and amino ($NH_3^+$) groups on amino acids and proteins. All ions carry either one (monovalent) or more (divalent, trivalent, etc.) positive or negative electrical charges.

Even pure water contains anions and cations because some water ($H_2O$) molecules dissociate into $H^+$'s and $OH^-$'s. How many do, depends primarily on temperature. The higher the temperature, the greater the dissociation of the water molecule and the higher the solution's concentrations of $H^+$ and $OH^-$. In complex aqueous solutions with many molecules, there are $H^+$ and $OH^-$ contributed just by dissociated water molecules themselves.

Although a volume of water may contain different kinds of cations and anions, the solution itself in a steady state is electrically neutral. The sum of electrical effects of all cations equals that of all anions, no matter their source, chemical nature, or charge strength. Though an aqueous solution is electrically neutral, it will have a predominant quality somewhere along the continuum from

> An acid increases a solution's [$H^+$]. A base decreases it.

acidity to alkalinity. For simple aqueous solutions, an acid is any material that when added to water ionizes to increase the [$H^+$]. A base is any material that ionizes to decrease [$H^+$]. These effects may occur directly if the dissociated molecule forms hydrogen ions, or indirectly if it promotes the dissociation of other molecules that do, like carbon dioxide.

All life processes depend on a well-regulated ratio between acids and bases in the body. But, living systems are not simple aqueous solutions. They are complex mixtures of water, some molecules of which are dissociated, that typically contain many additional molecules that are either dissolved, suspended, or ionized. All are mobile and move in the solution with varying degrees of freedom along concentration gradients for diffusion, by bulk flow along pressure gradients in convection, and along electrical gradients if they have an electrical charge.

Because of the diverse composition of watery solutions in living systems, their acid-base status must be defined in a more complex way than it is for pure water. For living systems, an acid is any material that increases $[H^+]$; a base decreases it. Molecules that dissociate and completely ionize in

> A "strong acid" is a molecule that completely dissociates in water to increase its $[H^+]$.

water lose not only their nascent molecular characteristics, they may directly affect the acid-base quality of the solution. For example, hydrochloric acid (HCl) in water dissociates to increase $[H^+]$ and $[Cl^-]$, thereby increasing the solution's acidity. HCl is considered to be a "strong acid" because it virtually dissociates completely in water. This is not because of the $H^+$ added by HCl itself, but because of the establishment of a "negative strong ion difference" in the solution, as described later.

Likewise, sodium hydroxide (NaOH) dissolved in water dissociates to increase $[Na^+]$ and $[OH^-]$, thereby decreasing the solution's $[H^+]$ and acidity. NaOH is a "strong base" because it dissociates nearly completely in water. The decrease in acidity is not because of the $OH^-$ contributed by dissociated

> A "strong ion" is one that remains in solution as an electrically charged element.

NaOH itself, but because of the establishment of a "positive strong ion difference" in the solution.

Other molecules also dissociate in water to affect its acidity, but only indirectly. For example, carbon dioxide ($CO_2$), a gas, dissolves in water ($[CO_2]_{dissolved}$), but also reacts with it to form carbonic acid ($H_2CO_3$) which dissociates to form $H^+$ and $HCO_3^-$. The net indirect effect is an increase in acidity. For this reason, carbon dioxide, a normal metabolic byproduct formed throughout the body, is called an acid.  More precisely, it increases only indirectly [$H^+$] in the body to increase its acidity.

Definitions for "acid" and "base" used in this book differ from those commonly presented by others.  The reason is simple, but important.  Many consider an acid to be a "proton donor" and a base to be a "proton acceptor," implying that adding $H^+$ 's to a solution is the same as adding acid to it.  This is the basic premise for the Bronsted-Lowry theory ( Fencl & Leith, 1993; Cohen & Kassirer, 1982).  It is impossible, of course,  to add only $H^+$ 's (protons) to a solution. In reality, any change in an aqueous solution's [$H^+$] is determined by a number of simultaneously acting physical and chemical constraints.  One constraint is that the solution itself remains electrically neutral.  The number of these constraints increase as the complexity of the solution increases.  The solution's [$H^+$] is a dependent, not an independent variable.  Further, the "donor-acceptor" definitions do not account for a solution being chemically neutral - the state of being neither acidic nor alkaline (Fencl & Leith, 1993; Rahn & Howell, 1978).

# Section D

## Main Points from Chapter 1

✔ A solution's $[H^+]$, as expressed in its pH measurement, depends on its concentrations of cations and anions, its dissolved carbon dioxide and other molecules.

✔ The number expressing measured pH of a solution is dimensionless (it has no units). It is the common logarithm of the reciprocal of the solution's $[H^+]$ in units of Eq/L.

✔ When a solution's $[H^+]$ increases, its pH decreases, and *vice versa*.

✔ Hydrogen ion is in trace amounts in most body fluids. Its concentration is typically expressed in units of "$10^{-9}$ Eq/L." ($1 \cdot 10^{-9}$ Eq/L = 1 nEq/L)

✔ Water has the highest concentration (at least 55 M/L) of any molecule in body fluids.

✔ Water molecules weakly dissociate to free hydrogen and hydroxyl ions. Its dissociation constant ($K_w$) depends on temperature and on the ionic strength of the solution.

✔ Each body fluid compartment has a discreet volume and ionic composition (Figure 1-2 and Table 1-2).

✔ An acid is a molecule that when added to water causes an increase in the solution's $[H^+]$ and a decrease in its pH.

✔ A base is a molecule that when added to water causes a decrease in the solution's $[H^+]$ and an increase in its pH.

✔ All aqueous solutions are electrically neutral, including body fluids.

# Chapter 2
## Ions in Aqueous Solutions

**What to Look for:**

In this chapter you will learn about:

- how molecules dissociate to form ions
- equilibrium constants for chemical reactions
- electrical neutrality of all solutions, including water
- strong molecules, acids and bases
- SID (a solution's "strong ion difference")
- calculating SID

Knowing about the physical chemical factors and forces that control ionization processes is essential for understanding the interactions among the many molecules and ions normally in body fluid compartments, including those circulating through the body in blood and plasma. This insight is the basis for seeing how $[H^+]$ is established and regulated in body fluids.

## Section A
### The Role of Molecular Dissociation to Form Ions

Many substances in aqueous solutions exist in two forms - as intact, unionized molecules and as the cations and anions they contribute to the solution when they dissociate.  The processes of ionization and reformation of the molecule are continuous, but balanced in a steady state as:

$$[intact\ molecule] \underset{k_2}{\overset{k_1}{\rightleftharpoons}} [ion_1] + [ion_2] \tag{1}$$

where:

[intact molecule] = concentration of undissociated molecule

$[ion_1]$, $[ion_2]$ = concentration of cations and anions contributed to the solution by the dissociation of the molecule

$k_1$, $k_2$ = rates of dissociation and molecular reformation, respectively.

The dissociation constant (K; also called "equilibrium constant" or "ionization constant") for a molecule is defined by the "Law of Mass Action" which states that the ratio between the product of the concentrations of the dissociated ions and the concentration of the undissociated (intact) molecule, is expressed as:

$$K = \frac{k_1}{k_2} = \frac{[ion_1] \times [ion_2]}{[intact\ molecule]} \tag{2}$$

# Section B

## Water

### B.1.  The Role of Water

Water is the diluent throughout the body in which all molecules and ions are either suspended, or dissolved.  Water as a molecule, however, also dissociates to affect the acid-base status of the solution because of the hydrogen ions it contributes.

For water (analogous to Equation 1):

$$[H_2O] \overset{k_1}{\underset{k_2}{\rightleftharpoons}} [H^+] + [OH^-] \tag{3}$$

and, analogous to Equation 2, its dissociation constant ($K_w$) is:

$$K_w = \frac{[H^+] \times [OH^-]}{[H_2O]} \tag{4}$$

and by rearrangement:

$$K_w \times [H_2O] = [H^+] \times [OH^-] \tag{5}$$

The concentration of undissociated water molecules (55.5 M/L) in a solution of pure water is several orders of magnitude greater than that of either $[H^+]$, or $[OH^-]$. This means that changes in the concentration of either of these ions has negligible effect either on the concentration of the undissociated molecule, $[H_2O]$, or on the product ($K_w \times [H_2O]$), so that a new constant, the "ion product of water" ($K'_w$; $(Eq/L)^2$), is defined as:

$$K'_w = [H^+] \times [OH^-] \tag{6}$$

$K'_w$ for pure water expresses an important relationship for how $[H^+]$ and $[OH^-]$

are balanced with the concentration of the undissociated water molecule ($H_2O$).

$K_w$, and therefore $K'_w$, increases with temperature so that both [$H^+$] and [$OH^-$] increase also, and *vice versa*. Since the concentrations of both ions

> Body water is a "weakly dissociated" molecule whose predominant concentration is in the molecular form "$H_2O$".

increase proportionately, electrical neutrality is maintained, regardless of temperature. Aqueous solutions maintain electrical neutrality in a similar way. Elevated temperature of incompletely dissociated (also called, "weakly dissociated") molecules in a solution increases cation and anion concentrations, but electrical neutrality is still preserved. This means that for an aqueous solution, the proportion of cations and anions contributed by a molecule which has dissociated remains constant and independent of temperature. The dissociation constants for molecules, however, vary with temperature. The importance of this effect is described in the next section.


## B.2. The Electrical Neutrality of Water


Electrical neutrality is established in pure water because [$H^+$] = [$OH^-$], so it is defined for water as:

$$[H^+] - [OH^-] = 0 \tag{7}$$

and,

$$[H^+] = \sqrt{K'_w} \tag{8}$$

Because $[H^+] = [OH^-]$, and $K'_w = [H^+] \times [OH^-]$, then by substitution, $K'_w = [H^+] \times [H^+]$, or $K'_w = [H^+]^2$, and $[H^+] = \sqrt{K'_w}$. By similar logic: $[OH^-] = \sqrt{K'_w}$.

Equation 7 defines both acid-base and electrical neutrality for pure water. Equation 8 derives from Equations 6 and 7 and is the basis for calculating $[H^+]$. These relationships are important for recognizing the error in the often-stated claim that, "The neutral pH for water is 7.0". The statement is true

> Water is acid-base neutral when $[H^+] = \sqrt{K'_w} = [OH^-]$. It is acidic when $[H^+] > \sqrt{K'_w} > [OH^-]$, and basic when $[H^+] < \sqrt{K'_w} < [OH^-]$

only when the water is at 25°C because $K'_w$ varies directly with temperature. When an aqueous solution increases its temperature, its $K'_w$ also increases and its pH for neutrality decreases, and *vice versa*. This effectively sets the point of acid-base neutrality for all solutions. Data in Figures 2-3 and 2-4 show how pH, $[H^+]$ and $[OH^-]$ for pure water vary as functions of temperature.

Data in Figures 2-3 and 2-4 show the importance for defining water's acid-base and electrical neutrality only in reference to its steady state temperature. There is a similar

> Pure water is both electrically and acid-base neutral, but its $[H^+]$ varies with temperature. The neutral point for water is at a pH of 7.0 only when it is at 25°C. It decreases when water temperature rises, and *vice versa*. At a body temperature of 37°C, it is 6.8.

temperature effect on aqueous solutions with many different ions and molecules, like body fluids. For example, a poikilotherm (a so-called "cold-blooded" animal) at 10°C has a markedly higher pH for acid-base neutrality, compared with its so-called "neutral pH" at room temperature (*viz.*, 25°C). It has accumulated more than 82% more $H^+$'s solely as a result of the higher body temperature (Figures 2-3 and 2-4).

Similarly, an animal at 37°C, a representative temperature for a homeotherm (a so-called "warm-blooded "animal), has a greater [H$^+$], compared to that at 30°C. The strong dependency of a molecule's dissociation constant on temperature is why a hypothermic person becomes progressively alkalotic as body temperature is reduced below its normal level (Rahn et.al., 1975; Rahn & Howell, 1978; Reeves, 1985; Swan, 1985). It also explains why someone becomes less alkalotic when body temperature goes, for example, from 30° C to 37° C.

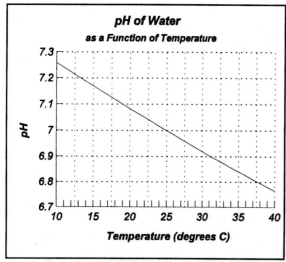

**Figure 2-3:** pH decreases for pure water as its temperature increases.

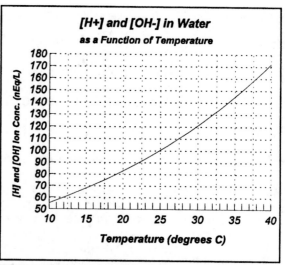

**Figure 2-4:** [H$^+$] and [OH$^-$] are equal and derive from the dissociation of water molecules which increase with temperature.

Even though body fluids inside cells have many different cation and anion species, the intracellular fluid itself is electrically neutral, as is the extracellular fluid. This doesn't imply, however, there are no differences in voltage in the body. Many cells maintain a voltage across their membranes, rapid transients in which give rise, for example to electrocardiograms (ECG's) and electroencephalograms (EEG's). In an aqueous solution, the proportional concentrations of cations and anions remain unchanged, so the solution itself is electrically neutral.

# Section C

## Strong Molecules, Acids, and Bases

Electrical neutrality in pure water (Equation 7) comes from its equal concentrations of a cationic ($H^+$) and anionic ($OH^-$) species. Electrical neutrality in aqueous solutions that contain other ions similarly comes from the equal concentrations of all its cations and all its anions. Body fluids, as for other aqueous solutions, typically contain many different electrolytes (ions) which come from diverse molecules, some of which are completely dissociated. Others are not.

Although all intact molecules change their physical state when they dissolve in water, they have different fates. Some, like glucose, for example, dissolve, but because they do not carry an electrical charge, they are neither ions, nor electrolytes. They are called "non-electrolytes." Others dissociate into components that have an electrical charge which remain stable in the solution as electrolytes. Yet others dissociate into components, some of which remain electrolytes, but others combine chemically to form new molecules. Only those molecules which dissolve in water to form electrolytes, affect the electrical state of the solution.

> Not all materials which dissolve in water add to its electrolyte concentration. Some combine with other molecules to form new compounds. Others are in a dissolved state, but do not have an electrical charge. They remain as non-electrolytes.

The words "strong" and "weak" are often used as adjectives to identify characteristics for a "molecule," an "acid," and a "base." Each has different meanings in the context of its use. A "strong molecule "is one that completely dissociates in a solution. For example a "strong acid," such as HCl, when added to water completely dissociates to form a cation ($H^+$) and an anion ($Cl^-$), which increases the solution's hydrogen ion concentration and thereby decreases its pH. A "strong

> Strong molecules, acids and bases have pK's less than 4.0. Their molecules completely dissociate in aqueous solutions.

base,"as for example NaOH, also completely dissociates in water to form a cation ($Na^+$) and anion ($OH^-$), which causes the solution's hydrogen ion concentration to decrease and thereby increase its pH.

An aqueous solution to which a strong molecule is added has little, if any, of the undissociated molecule remaining in solution once it has dissociated. The judgement of whether a molecule is "strong" or "weak" rests on the extent to which it dissociates in water, as defined by its dissociation constant (K; Eq/L) and expressed by its pK, which is the "common" logarithm (to base 10) of the reciprocal of K. By convention, a strong molecule, acid or base is one that has a dissociation constant (K) greater than $1 \times 10^{-4}$ Eq/L (pK < 4). HCl, $H_2SO_4$, NaOH and NaCl are molecules that so strongly dissociate, their pK's are unmeasurably small (their K is extremely large).

A weak molecule, acid or base is one that only partially dissociates and has a dissociation constant (K) less than $1 \times 10^{-4}$ Eq/L (pK > 4). An aqueous solution containing a weak molecule is a mixture of the undissociated molecule and its dissociated ions

> Weak molecules, acids and bases have pK's greater than 4.0. The parent molecule and its dissociated ions coexist in the solution.

(Equation 2). Water itself is a very weakly dissociated molecule (K = $1.82 \times 10^{-16}$ Eq/L; pK = 15.7 at 25°C). Few water molecules dissociate to add to a solution's

$H^+$ and $OH^-$ concentrations. Similarly, $H_2PO_4^-$ , a weak anion, dissociates to form a $H^+$ and $HPO_4^{2-}$. The parent and dissociated ions coexist in an aqueous solution.

## C.1. Strong Ions or Electrolytes

A "strong ion" remains as an ion in a solution and does not chemically react with other molecules or ions. For example, dissolved NaCl completely dissociates into a strong cation ($Na^+$) and a strong anion ($Cl^-$), both of which remain as ions in the solution; they do not react with each other to form the salt NaCl,

> A "strong ion" does not chemically react with other molecules or ions in a solution. It remains as a freely mobile particle with one or more, positive or negative electrical charges.

or with the $H^+$ or $OH^-$ from dissociated water to form NaOH or HCl. Likewise, $Na_2SO_4$ in water dissociates completely into two $Na^+$'s and a $SO_4^{2-}$ and both remain as ions in the solution.

Conversely, HCl added to water dissociates into $H^+$'s and $Cl^-$'s. These $H^+$'s disrupt the equilibrium reaction of water, so that some react with the $OH^-$'s from water to reestablish the water equilibrium. The net effect is to increase the $[H^+]$ of the solution, but this increase is less than those added by the HCl itself. The $Cl^-$, however, remains in solution as a "strong ion," decreasing the strong ion difference and causing $[H^+]$ to increase. This makes the solution more acidic. When NaOH is added to water, the dissociated $Na^+$'s remain in solution as "strong ions" while some $OH^-$'s react with the $H^+$'s from water dissociation to reform water. The net effect of the increased $[Na^+]$ is to increase the strong ion difference and cause the solution's $[H^+]$ to decrease. This makes the solution less acidic.

A strong ion's electrical charge defines how it affects the solution's acid-base character. For example, strong cations are "basic cations" because they reduce the solution's [H$^+$]. Strong anions are "acidic anions" because

> Positively charged strong ions reduce [H$^+$]. They are called, "basic cations". Negatively charged strong ions increase [H$^+$]. They are called, "acidic anions".

they increase the solution's [H$^+$] Na$^+$, K$^+$, Mg$^{2+}$ and Ca$^{2+}$ are the most common basic cations in biological solutions. Cl$^-$, SO$_4^{2-}$, and a few organic acid anions like lactate$^-$ ( K = 1.38x10$^{-4}$ Eq/L; pK = 3.86) are common acidic anions.

## C.2. The Strong Ion Difference ([SID])

The acid-base status of a solution depends in part on the net difference in the concentration between its strong cations and its strong anions (commonly expressed in units of Eq/L), but not on the ionic species itself. The net electrical charge for all of the strong ions can be positive, negative or zero. The "strong ion difference" ([SID]) for a solution is defined as:

$$[SID] = \Sigma (strong\ cations) - \Sigma (strong\ anions) \qquad (9)$$

but, the entire solution is electrically neutral because when it contains only strong ions and water:

$$[H^+] - [OH^-] \pm [SID] = 0 \qquad (10)$$

## C.3. [SID] and Acid-Base Neutrality

Any solution other than pure water is a mixture of strong and weak cations, and strong and weak anions. They are contributed by dissociated molecules in a solution of predominantly undissociated water molecules. For all solutions, electrical neutrality is always maintained. One way or another, the total concentration of anions eventually comes to equal that of cations. This is a thermodynamic obligation for all solutions. In addition, for an aqueous solution with only strong ions, some have a neutral pH (i.e., $[OH^-] = [H^+]$), some are acidic and some are basic. Those that are acidic have a greater $[H^+]$ than do those with a neutral pH. Those that are basic have a lesser $[H^+]$ than do those with a neutral pH. Nevertheless, all are electrically neutral.

For example, NaCl dissolved in water completely dissociates to form strong cations ($Na^+$) and strong anions ($Cl^-$). Both ion species are equally concentrated and each has the same valence. The solution remains at a

> Just $[H^+]$ or pH are not the only determinants of a solution's acidity, alkalinity, or neutrality. The acid-base status of an aqueous solution containing strong ions also depends in part on its [SID] and on its temperature.

neutral pH because the ratio of $[H^+]$ and $[OH^-]$ remains unchanged from that of pure water. Also, there is no difference between the concentrations of the strong ions $Na^+$ and $Cl^-$. The strong ion difference is zero. This is an example of a solution that is electrically neutral and one that remains at a neutral pH.

Some solutions do not retain acid-base neutrality, although they remain electrically neutral. Hydrochloric acid when added to water dissociates to form $H^+$'s and $Cl^-$'s. Some of the excess $H^+$'s will combine with $OH^-$'s of dissociated water molecules to form neutral water. The $Cl^-$'s remain as free ions. The solution now has strong anions ($Cl^-$'s) whose concentration is not matched by strong cations. Electrical neutrality is maintained, but the solution has a greater concentration of $H^+$'s than there was in the pure water, so it has a lower pH and is acidic. Also, there is a greater concentration of $Cl^-$ than in pure water.

This establishes a so-called, "negative SID", meaning that there is a strong ion difference with a predominance of a strong anion (Fig. 2- 5). For this solution, the greater the concentration of the strong anion, $Cl^-$, the greater is its final acidity, and *vice versa*. This is an example of a solution that is electrically neutral and one that has a higher $[H^+]$ because of the predominance of a strong acidic anion.

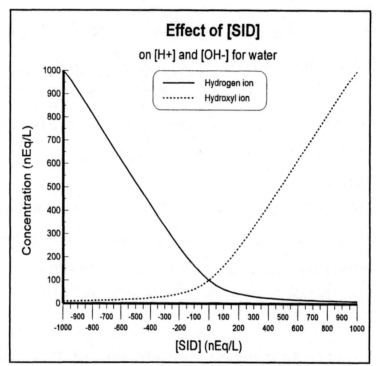

**Figure 2-5:** The "strong ion difference" (SID) determines the ratio of hydrogen and hydroxyl ions through the dissociation of water molecules.

In contrast, an electrically neutral solution can become basic by having a $[H^+]$ less than a solution that is acid-base neutral and has a "positive [SID]", as shown in Figure 2-5. For example, NaOH dissolves in pure water to dissociate completely to produce strong cations ($Na^+$'s) and weak anions ($OH^-$'s). [SID] is positive because the solution has a high concentration of strong cations with no matched concentration of strong anions. This affects the dissociation constant for water so that more water molecules form at the expense of reducing the solution's [$H^+$]. The solution is electrically neutral, but has a higher pH than pure water and is basic. For this solution, the greater the concentration of the strong cation, $Na^+$, the greater is its final alkalinity, and *vice versa*. This is an example of a solution that is electrically neutral and one that has a lower [$H^+$] than pure water because of the predominance of a strong basic cation.

The strong ion difference in an aqueous solution directs its acidity or its alkalinity depending on the predominance of its net strong ion difference for anions (acidity) or cations (alkalinity). It does this regardless of the

A solution's strong ion difference ([SID]) is a powerful factor in determining its acid-base status. The greater [SID] is positive, the less will be its hydrogen ion concentration and the more the solution will be alkaline. The greater [SID] is negative, the higher will be its hydrogen ion concentration and the more it will be acidic.

number of strong cationic or strong anionic species in the solution, but as a function of their net differences in concentration.

# Section D

## Calculating [$H^+$] and [$OH^-$] with [SID]

The [$H^+$] and [$OH^-$] of an aqueous solution containing strong ions depends on its [SID]. Its electrical neutrality is defined by Equation 10. Solving Equation 6 for

[OH$^-$] shows that [OH$^-$] = K$'_w$ /[H$^+$], so that:

$$[H^+] + [SID] - \frac{K'_w}{[H^+]} = 0 \tag{11}$$

Multiplying both sides of Equation 11 by [H$^+$] produces:

$$[H^+]^2 + [SID] \cdot [H^+] - K'_w = 0 \tag{12}$$

which is a quadratic equation with the general form:

$$A \cdot X^2 + B \cdot X + C = 0 \tag{13}$$

whose solution is:

$$X = \frac{\sqrt{B^2 - 4 \cdot A \cdot C}}{2 \cdot A} - \frac{B}{2 \cdot A} \tag{14}$$

When X = [H$^+$], A = 1, B = [SID], and C = K$'_w$ because in Equation 12 the ion product of water is expressed as "- K$'_w$", then in Equation 14, "-4 •(- K$'_w$)" is expressed as "+4 • K$'_w$" and,

$$[H^+] = \frac{\sqrt{[SID]^2 + 4 \cdot K'_w} - [SID]}{2} \tag{15}$$

By a similar process, solving Equation 6 for $[H^+]$ shows that:

$$[OH^-] = \frac{\sqrt{[SID]^2 + 4 \cdot K'_w} + [SID]}{2} \qquad (16)$$

As a general principle for any aqueous solution containing strong ions at electrical neutrality:

1) the greater the strong ion difference in favor of strong cations, the less will be its $[H^+]$, the higher will be its pH, and the more it will be basic, and

2) the greater the strong ion difference in favor of strong anions, the greater will be its $[H^+]$, the lower will be its pH, and the more it will be acidic.

Acid-base neutrality is dependent on temperature because the equilibrium of water dissociation ($K_w$) is dependent on temperature. As temperature increases, $K_w$ and therefore $K'_w$ increase causing both $[H^+]$ and $[OH^-]$ to increase and acid-base neutral pH to decrease, and *vice versa*.

This chapter presents the effects of only the first of three independent variables which define the acid-base status of an aqueous solution, that of its strong ion difference ($[SID]$). The effects of dissolved carbon dioxide and non-volatile weak acids are described next.

# Section E

## Main Points from Chapter 2

✔   *The Law of Mass Action* states that the rate of a chemical reaction is proportional to the concentrations of the reacting substances.  It defines the equilibrium constant for the reaction.  Equation 2 is a general expression of this law. Equations 5 and 6 show its application for pure water.

✔   *The Law of Electrical Neutrality* states that for any macroscopic sample of an aqueous solution, the sum of all the cation concentrations must equal the sum of all anion concentrations (i.e., $\Sigma$ [cations]) - $\Sigma$ [anions]) = 0), so the solution is always electrically neutral.  Equation 7 is an expression of this law for pure water.

✔   Applications of *The Law of Mass Action* and *The Law of Electrical Neutrality* to pure  water, define its acid-base status with reference to $K'_w$ .

        a) Water is acid-base neutral when $[H^+] = \sqrt{K'_w} = [OH^-]$

        b) Water is acidic when $[H^+] > \sqrt{K'_w} > [OH^-]$

        c) Water is basic when $[H^+] < \sqrt{K'_w} < [OH^-]$

✔   Similar to pH, a value of pK is a dimensionless number.  It is calculated as the common logarithm of the reciprocal of the dissociation constant (K; Eq/L), i.e., pK = log (1/K).

✔     A strong molecule, acid or base has a dissociation constant (K) greater than $1 \times 10^{-4}$ Eq/L, that is, it has a pK less than 4.0. The molecule in solution dissociates into its ions.

✔     A weak molecule, acid or base has a dissociation constant (K) less than $1 \times 10^{-4}$ Eq/L, that is, it has a pK greater than 4.0. Both the undissociated molecule and its ions coexist in solution.

✔     A strong ion does not chemically react with other molecules or ions in the solution. $Na^+$, $K^+$, $Ca^{2+}$ and $Mg^{2+}$ are strong cations in body fluids. Strong anions in body fluids are: $Cl^-$, lactate$^-$ and $SO_4^{2-}$.

✔     Equation 9 defines the strong ion difference ([SID]) for a solution. It is positive when there is an excess of strong cations, and negative when there is an excess of strong anions. [SID] is zero when [strong cations] = [strong anions].

✔     Equation 15 defines [$H^+$] and equation 16 defines [$OH^-$] for any aqueous solution containing only strong ions. Both [$H^+$] and [$OH^-$] are dependent variables, determined by the independent variable [SID] and a constant ($K'_w$).

✔     [SID] is usually expressed in units of mEq/L for biological solutions (see Table 1-2) and is much larger than $\sqrt{K'_w}$ . Equations 15 & 16 and Figure 2-5 show that in an aqueous solution containing strong ions:

     a) when [SID] is positive, [$OH^-$] = [SID]; [$H^+$] = $K'_w$ /[SID].

     b) when [SID] is negative, [$H^+$] = -[SID]; [$OH^-$] = $K'_w$ /-[SID].

# Chapter 3
## The "$CO_2$ System"

**What to Look for:**

In this chapter you will learn about:

- the importance of alveolar ventilation in setting $[H^+]$
- the different molecular forms of carbon dioxide in the body
- the different chemical reactions that affect how carbon dioxide is stored
- how carbon dioxide changes its phase state in setting acid-base status
- how carbon dioxide functions as an acid in body fluids

All oxidative metabolic processes produce carbon dioxide as a byproduct of their conversion of foodstuffs to energy. Some of this energy appears either as heat, as physical movements, or it is stored by the processes of growth and repair.

Normal acid-base status is most commonly challenged by exercise. Whole body metabolic rate with its production of $CO_2$ typically increases as much as seven-fold with peaks in

> Increases in alveolar ventilation normally reduce quickly the body's increase in $[H^+]$ with exercise by expelling carbon dioxide as a gas to the atmosphere.

physical activity, sometimes even more, over rest levels of about 200 ml/min. The indirect formation of H$^+$ linked to such high rates of metabolically produced CO$_2$ increases [H$^+$] and acidity in blood and in other body fluids. As PCO$_2$ and [H$^+$] increase, however, alveolar ventilation ($\dot{V}_A$) normally increases reflexly to promote the loss of CO$_2$ as a gas at the alveolar membrane. The partial pressure gradient between CO$_2$ dissolved in alveolar capillary blood and that in alveolar gas promotes its rapid diffusion into airway spaces from which it is exhaled. This is an important mechanism for moment-to-moment acid-base adjustments.

Substantial increases in CO$_2$ and [H$^+$] also occur with exercise-induced or environmentally-induced hyperthermia, or fever when metabolic rates increase because of the elevation in tissue temperature. Similarly, metabolic rate and H$^+$ production fall with hypothermia.

Carbon dioxide does not have a first-order effect on [H$^+$] because the molecule itself does not add hydrogen ions to the solution when it dissolves. Its effect is secondary through the "CO$_2$ system". The "CO$_2$ system" (Figure 3-6) is a series of reversible reactions between (CO$_2$)$_{gas}$ in the lungs and the different forms of CO$_2$ in blood and other body fluids. An increase in dissolved carbon dioxide causes

> Dissolved carbon dioxide has the effect of being an acid in an aqueous solution only through its relationships in the "CO$_2$ system".

many of its reactions in blood and body fluids to increase Carbon dioxide (CO$_2$) is an acid, as defined in Chapter 1, because adding it to water increases its hydrogen ion concentration even though indirectly.

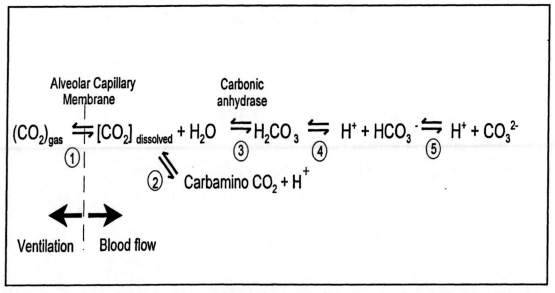

**Figure 3-6: The "CO₂ System"** Carbon dioxide as a gas in the alveoli is in equilibrium with that in the blood (Reaction No. 1). Some dissolved $CO_2$ reacts with amino groups on proteins to form "carbamino $CO_2$" (Reaction No.2). More dissolved $CO_2$, however, combines with water (catalyzed by carbonic anhydrase in most fluid compartments; but not in plasma) to form carbonic acid ($H_2CO_3$ ; Reaction No. 3), which rapidly dissociates into $H^+$ and $HCO_3^-$ (Reaction No. 4). Some of the $HCO_3^-$ dissociates to form $H^+$ and carbonate ($CO_3^{2-}$; Reaction No. 5).

# Section A

## The Role of Respiration

Because the fraction of $CO_2$ in the atmosphere (that in inspired gas, $F_I CO_2$) is less than 1% it doesn't contribute to the body's dissolved $CO_2$. Metabolic processes are the sole source of $CO_2$. The rate of carbon dioxide production ($\dot{V}CO_2$) by the body is calculated as the product of expired minute ventilation and the expired fraction of $CO_2$ (e.g. $\dot{V}_E \bullet F_E CO_2$). In a steady state (i.e. when ventilation and gas fractions are constant), the expression ($\dot{V}_A \bullet F_A CO_2$) is a function of the product ($\dot{V}_E \bullet F_E CO_2$). Body carbon dioxide production rate is expressed as:

$$\dot{V}CO_2 = \dot{V}_A \cdot F_A CO_2 \qquad (17)$$

where:

$\dot{V}CO_2$ = CO$_2$ production rate (ml/min; STPD)

$\dot{V}_A$ = Alveolar ventilation (L/min; BTPS)

$F_A CO_2$ = Fraction of CO$_2$ in alveolar gas (% CO$_2$ /100)

The fraction of CO$_2$ is related to the partial pressure of CO$_2$ by:

$$F_A CO_2 = \frac{P_A CO_2}{P_B - P_{H_2O}} \qquad (18)$$

where:

$P_A CO_2$ = partial pressure of CO$_2$ in alveolar gas (Torr)

$P_B$ = barometric pressure (Torr)

$P_{H2O}$ = partial pressure of water at body temperature (37°C; 47 Torr)

Because the alveolar partial pressure of CO$_2$ ($P_A CO_2$ in Equation 18) is equal to the partial pressure of CO$_2$ in systemic arterial blood ($P_a CO_2$), the term $P_A CO_2$ is replaced by $P_a CO_2$ in Equation 18 (West, 1995) and Equation 17 is rewritten as:

$$\dot{V}CO_2 = \dot{V}_A \cdot \frac{P_a CO_2}{P_B - P_{H_2O}} \qquad (19)$$

and rearranging:

$$\dot{V}_A = \frac{\dot{V}CO_2 \cdot (P_B - P_{H_2O})}{P_aCO_2}$$ (20)

In a steady state, carbon dioxide production rate is constant, as are the other factors in the numerator of Equation 20. The partial pressure of $CO_2$ in systemic arterial blood is inversely related to alveolar ventilation so that $PaCO_2$ varies with alveolar ventilation. A higher than normal $PaCO_2$ (hypercapnia) is caused by an inadequate alveolar ventilation (hypoventilation). A lower than normal $PaCO_2$ (hypocapnia) is caused by hyperventilation.

Carbon dioxide is a gas in the lungs, but it is dissolved in body fluids. Even so, the concentration of dissolved $CO_2$ is often expressed as a partial pressure. This implies an equilibrium between dissolved $CO_2$ in a fluid and that in an overlying gas with that partial pressure. A fluid's total $CO_2$ is the sum of that which is soluble in and freely diffusible across membranes, $(CO_2)_{dissolved}$, and that in molecular combinations as $H_2CO_3$, $HCO_3^-$, $CO_3^{2-}$ and carbamino $CO_2$ (Figure 3-6).

> The concentration of dissolved carbon dioxide is expressed as a partial pressure. This indicates its equilibrium point were it exposed to a gas with that partial pressure.

Both voluntary and reflex changes in respiration quickly affect the dissolved carbon dioxide ($PCO_2$) in all tissues and that in circulating systemic arterial blood ($P_aCO_2$). A decrease in $P_aCO_2$, that in circulating systemic arterial blood ($P_aCO_2$). A decrease in

> Hyperventilation removes carbon dioxide from plasma, which secondarily causes a rise in body fluid pH and induces alkalosis. Hypoventilation has the opposite effect, resulting in acidosis.

$P_aCO_2$, for example during hyperventilation, steepens the partial pressure $CO_2$ gradient between circulating blood and the tissues through which it flows. $CO_2$ is lost from tissue which then decreases its [H+] and increases its pH. This induces a so-called "respiratory alkalosis". An increase in $P_aCO_2$, as by hypoventilation, has the opposite effect, resulting in a so-called "respiratory acidosis". Any compartment and tissue which undergoes these changes depends on its volume flow rate of arterial blood. How great the change is depends on a steady state between the rate of carbon dioxide production by cellular metabolism and the rate of the tissue's blood perfusion. Respiratory reflexes normally adjust alveolar ventilation to provide these rapid and precise acid-base adjustments.

Because of the way in which alveolar ventilation affects the body's $PCO_2$ (or $[CO_2]_{dissolved}$), the concentrations of hydrogen, bicarbonate and other ions and molecules depend on $P_ACO_2$ and on the "$CO_2$ system". This means that the $PCO_2$ of any body fluid is adjusted by alveolar ventilation. This is why it is often stated that, "body fluid compartments are open to the

> The loss of carbon dioxide through lung ventilation affects [H+] throughout the body.

atmosphere" and their $PCO_2$ is adjusted as an independent control variable. With any maintained level of $CO_2$ production ($\dot{V}CO_2$), the numerator of Equation 20 is a constant. Alveolar ventilation ($\dot{V}_A$) and $P_aCO_2$ are reciprocally related to regulate $PCO_2$ and [H+] in each of the body fluid compartments. Respiratory alkalosis or acidosis develop when this regulation is impaired.

## Section B

### Carbon Dioxide in Solution

The total amount of $CO_2$ in body fluids is predominantly represented by the sum of dissolved $CO_2$ and $HCO_3^-$, with diminishingly smaller amounts of $CO_3^{2-}$ ( Figure 3-6, Reaction #5) , $H_2CO_3$ ( Reaction #3) and carbamino $CO_2$ ( R-NHCOO⁻; Reaction #2). Some $CO_2$ is lost from blood by diffusion at the alveolar capillary membrane to gas in the alveoli from which it is subsequently expired by ventilation.

> A body fluid's total carbon dioxide is represented largely by that combined in bicarbonate ions and that dissolved in the fluid.

Carbon dioxide is a very soluble and rapidly diffusing molecule which not only quickly distributes itself along partial pressure gradients throughout cells and body fluids, but which also is transformed into other molecules and ions (Figure 3-6). As soon as it is produced by metabolism, it dissolves in intracellular fluid rapidly because of its relatively high solubility coefficient, assumed to be close to that of plasma ($\alpha_{CO2}$ = 3.1 x 10⁻⁵ Eq/L•Torr⁻¹ at 37°C), diffuses into extracellular body fluids and returns to the lungs where $[CO_2]_{dissolved}$ exchanges with $(CO_2)_{gas}$ in the lung alveoli (Figure 3-6, Reaction #1). The $[CO_2]_{dissolved}$ is calculated using Henry's Law as:

$$[CO_2]_{dissolved} = \alpha_{CO2} \cdot PCO_2 \qquad (21)$$

where:

$[CO_2]_{dissolved}$ = concentration of dissolved $CO_2$ (M/L)

$\alpha_{CO2}$ = solubility of $CO_2$ in plasma @37°C (3.1 • 10⁻⁵ M/L· Torr⁻¹

$PCO_2$ = partial pressure of $CO_2$ in plasma

The majority of $[CO_2]_{dissolved}$ chemically combines quickly with water to form carbonic acid ($H_2CO_3$), when the reaction is catalyzed by the enzyme carbonic anhydrase (Figure 3-6, Reaction #3), as it is in tissues and the red blood cell. In a

similarly rapid manner, nearly all $H_2CO_3$ dissociates to form $H^+$ and $HCO_3^-$.
Reaction #3 is slow in plasma because there is no carbonic anhydrase.  When
Reactions 3 and 4 (Figure 3-6) are combined, and because of the Law of Mass
Action:

$$[H^+] \cdot [HCO_3^-] = K_c \cdot PCO_2 \qquad (22)$$

where:

$[H^+]$ = hydrogen ion concentration (Eq/L)

$[HCO_3^-]$ = bicarbonate concentration (Eq/L)

$PCO_2$ = partial pressure of $CO_2$ (Torr)

$K_c$ = $2.46 \cdot 10^{-11}$ (Eq/L)² · Torr⁻¹ @37°C (Fencl & Leith, 1993)

Because $H_2CO_3$ quickly dissociates and cannot be directly measured in body
fluids, $K_c$ represents the combined effects of an equilibrium constant ($K_{eq}$ =
$7.943 \cdot 10^{-7}$ Eq/L) and a solubility coefficient ($\alpha_{CO_2}$ = $3.1 \cdot 10^{-5}$ M/L · Torr⁻¹ ) for
the reaction: $[CO_2]_{dissolved}$ + $[H_2O]$ ⇌ $[H^+]$ + $[HCO_3^-]$.  It defines the rate of this
transformation .

A small amount of  $HCO_3^-$ subsequently dissociates to form $CO_3^{2-}$ (Figure 3-6,
Reaction #5), and because of the Law of Mass Action:

$$[H^+] \cdot [CO_3^{2-}] = K_3 \cdot [HCO_3^-] \qquad (23)$$

where:

$[CO_3^{2-}]$ = carbonate ion concentration (Eq/L)

$K_3$ = $6.0 \cdot 10^{-11}$ Eq/L @ 37°C ( Stewart, 1981)

Bicarbonate ion is often  assumed to have an important role in determining acid-base status, but its concentration in an aqueous solution cannot be measured

directly (Cohen & Kassirer, 1982;

Chinard, 1966). What is typically

assessed is total $CO_2$ concentration by

adding a strong acid to the solution,

forcing all of the reactions in Figure 3-6

> Hydrogen ion concentration in body fluids, and consequently their pH, is a dynamically established dependent variable.

to the left, releasing $CO_2$ as a gas. The total $CO_2$ concentration is then determined

manometrically or by assessing the change in pH of a buffer solution containing an

indicator dye (Cohen & Kassirer, 1982). Alternatively, a value for $[HCO_3^-]$ is

calculated from measured pH and $PCO_2$ using the Henderson-Hasselbalch equation:

$$pH = pK^I + Log \ \frac{[HCO_3^-]}{\alpha_{CO2} \bullet PCO_2} \tag{24}$$

Not many textbooks or other references explicitly state how bicarbonate ion

concentration is determined or whether it is assumed to be equivalent to total $CO_2$.

## Section C

### The Prime Determinants of $[H^+]$

All aqueous solutions, even those with complex and diverse constituents, are at

electrical neutrality. In such a uniform volume conductor, the sum of all cation

concentrations equals that of its anions. Hydrogen ion concentration is a

dynamically established dependent variable in this environment. In body fluids, like

interstitial fluid, cerebrospinal fluid, gastric juice and pancreatic juice, which

normally do not contain high concentrations of protein or phosphate, it is set by

the steady state relationship between the effects of two independent variables, the strong ion difference ([SID]) and $PCO_2$.

Even in such molecularly and ionically complex and time-varying solutions as body fluids, acid-base status still depends on water and its dissolved components. For example, in pure water, $[H^+]$ equals $[OH^-]$, so that, as stated in Equation 7 (Chapter 2), $[H^+]-[OH^-]=0$. Also, for aqueous solutions in which there is a strong ion difference, as stated in Equation 10 (Chapter 2), $[H^+] - [OH^-] \pm [SID] = 0$. Further, if the solution has a strong ion difference because of a predominance of strong anions, (i.e. $[H^+] - [OH^-] - [SID] = 0$), then its total anionic concentration is the sum of $[OH^-]$ and

[SID]. To maintain electrical neutrality, the solution's $[H^+]$ is higher than for pure water, so it is relatively acidic. There is an opposite

All aqueous solutions are electrically neutral. Those with a small positive or a negative SID because of a predominance of strong anions achieve this by having a high $[H^+]$ and are consequently acidic. Those with a large positive [SID] because of a predominance of strong cations achieve electrical neutrality by having a low $[H^+]$ and are consequently alkaline.

state when [SID] reflects a predominance of strong cations, (i.e. $[H^+] - [OH] + [SID] = 0$). The solution's total cation concentration is the sum of [SID] and $[H^+]$. For electrical neutrality, $[H^+]$ is lower than that of pure water and the solution is relatively basic, as are most body fluids except gastric juice.

Hydrogen ion concentration of an aqueous solution with a strong ion difference to which $CO_2$ has been added, as by a metabolic process, requires more complex analysis. For electrical neutrality such a solution's ionic concentrations are:

$$[H^+] + [SID] - [OH^-] - [HCO_3^-] - [CO_3^{2-}] = 0 \qquad (25)$$

Equation 25 shows that analyzing the acid-base status of an aqueous solution using only the Henderson-Hasselbalch equation is inescapably incomplete, because only hydrogen and bicarbonate ions are represented in Equation 24. It does not evaluate the net effect of completely dissociated strong electrolytes ([SID]; an independent variable) in the solution. In addition to $H^+$ and $HCO_3^-$, two other weak electrolytes, $OH^-$ and $CO_3^{2-}$, the concentrations of which are restrained by dissociation equilibria and the final requirement for the solution's electrical neutrality. Earlier analyses may have ignored the effects of $[OH^-]$ and $[CO_3^{2-}]$ for two reasons. They normally have only minor effects in determining acid-base status and, as for $[HCO_3^-]$, they can not be measured directly. But they can be calculated by:

Solving Equation 6 (Chapter 1; i.e., $[H^+] \bullet [OH^-] = K'_w$): $[OH^-] = K'_w /[H^+]$, then

$$[H^+] + [SID] - \frac{K'_w}{[H^+]} - [HCO_3^-] - [CO_3^{2-}] = 0 \qquad (26)$$

From Equation 22, $[HCO_3^-] = ( K_c \bullet PCO_2)/[H^+]$, and substituting in Equation 26:

$$[H^+] + [SID] - \frac{K'_w}{[H^+]} - \frac{K_c \bullet PCO_2}{[H^+]} - [CO_3^{2-}] = 0 \qquad (27)$$

From Equation 23, $[H^+] \bullet [CO_3^{2-}] = K_3 \bullet [HCO_3^-]$ and because $[HCO_3^-] = K_c \bullet PCO_2/ [H^+]$, then $[CO_3^{2-}] = K_3 \bullet Kc \bullet PCO_2/[H^+]^2$, and substituting in Equation 27:

$$[H^+] + [SID] - \frac{K'_w}{[H^+]} - \frac{K_c \bullet PCO_2}{[H^+]} - \frac{K_3 \bullet K_c \bullet PCO_2}{[H^+]^2} = 0 \qquad (28)$$

The equation for electrical neutrality (Equation 28) indicates that the dependent variable $[H^+]$ is the common factor which links water dissociation, bicarbonate and carbonate formation. This means that hydrogen ion is involved as a dependent variable in the reactions involving the other dependent variables (e.g. hydroxide, bicarbonate and carbonate ions). It does not mean that hydrogen ion is an independent variable determining [OH⁻], [HCO₃⁻] and/or [CO₃²⁻]. Whereas hydrogen, hydroxyl, bicarbonate and carbonate ions are dependent variables, intrinsic to a biological solution, $PCO_2$ and [SID] are independent variables and lever extrinsic influences on the solution, as indicated in Equation 29.

Multiplying both sides of Equation 28 by $[H^+]^2$, yields:

$$[H^+]^3 + [SID] \cdot [H^+]^2 - (K'_w + K_c \cdot PCO_2) \cdot [H^+] - (K_3 \cdot K_c \cdot PCO_2) = 0 \quad (29)$$

Equation 29 indicates that in body solutions containing only $CO_2$ and strong ions (for example, interstitial fluid , cerebrospinal fluid, gastric and pancreatic juice), the concentrations of its dependent variables H⁺, OH⁻, HCO₃⁻ and CO₃²⁻ are determined by two independent variables, $PCO_2$ and [SID]. An important inference from Equation 29 is that when either $PCO_2$ or [SID] changes in a biological solution, the effects are not only on its hydrogen ion concentration (shown in Figure 3-7) but also on its hydroxyl,

> In aqueous solutions, like body fluids, which contain strong ions and $CO_2$, [H⁺] varies as a function of two, independent variables, [SID] and $PCO_2$.

carbonate and bicarbonate concentrations as well. This is not so often concluded by those who depend on the Henderson-Hasselbalch equation (Equation 24) for analyses.

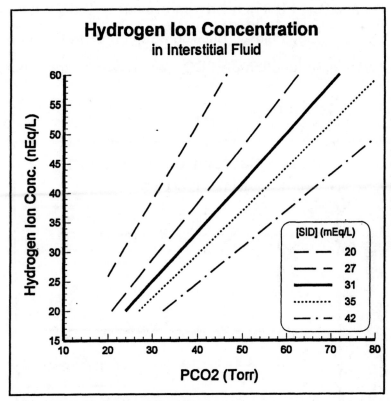

**Figure 3-7:** [H$^+$] in interstitial fluid varies as a function of PCO₂, but it also depends on [SID]. Representatively, a normal value for [H$^+$] is about 43 nEq/L when PCO₂ is about 50 Torr and [SID] is 31 mEq/L (solid line).

# Section D

## Protein-Free Solutions

Interstitial fluid, cerebrospinal fluid, gastric and pancreatic juice (Chapter 5) have negligible amounts of protein. The dependent variable, [H$^+$], in these fluids is determined by the two independent variables, [SID] and PCO$_2$ (Equation 29). Because [HCO$_3^-$] (Total CO$_2$) is in high concentration,

> In body fluids which contain negligible concentrations of protein, like interstitial fluid or gastric juice, [H$^+$], [HCO$_3^-$], [CO$_3^{2-}$] and [OH$^-$] are dependent variables. PCO$_2$ and [SID] are independent variables in them.

compared to [OH⁻] and [CO₃²⁻], it is nearly equivalent to [SID] when [SID] is positive, as it is in most body fluids. Bicarbonate concentration in a protein-free solution does not vary as a function of $PCO_2$ ,as shown by the relationships in Figure 3-8.

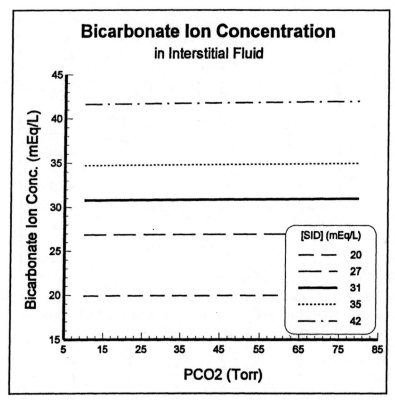

**Figure 3-8:** [HCO₃⁻] in interstitial fluid varies only slightly as a function of $PCO_2$. It is set primarily by [SID].

Substituting [SID] for [HCO₃⁻] in Equation 22 and rearranging to solve for [H⁺]:

$$[H^+] = K_c \cdot \frac{PCO_2}{[SID]}$$

(30)

and

$$\log \frac{1}{[H^+]} = \log \frac{1}{K_c} + \log \frac{[SID]}{PCO_2} \tag{31}$$

or,

$$pH = 10.6 + \log \frac{[SID]}{PCO_2} \tag{32}$$

In Equation 32 [SID] has units of Eq/L and PCO$_2$ has units of Torr. If [SID] has units of mEq/L, then:

$$pH = 7.6 + \log \frac{[SID]}{PCO_2} \tag{33}$$

Equation 30 is similar to Henderson's equation ( Henderson, 1928; Jones, 1987) and Equation 33 is similar to the Henderson-Hasselbalch equation (Equation 24;Astrup & Severinghaus, 1986; Fencl & Leith, 1993).

Equations 30 and 33 show, however, how two independent variables, [SID] and PCO$_2$ set [H$^+$] or pH, a dependent variable in protein-free solutions in which [SID] is positive and PCO$_2$ is in a physiological range.

## Section E

## Main Points from Chapter 3

✔    Metabolic processes are the sole source of the body's carbon dioxide.
Inspired air contains no carbon dioxide.

✔    Carbon dioxide is a gas only in the lung's airways and alveoli.  It is expelled
from the body by ventilation of the pulmonary alveoli.

✔    In a metabolic steady state (i.e. $\dot{V}CO_2$ is constant),  the partial pressure of
$CO_2$ in systemic arterial blood ($P_aCO_2$) is inversely related to alveolar
ventilation ($\dot{V}_A$) (Equation 20).

✔    Carbon dioxide is dissolved in body fluids.  It has the effect of being a weak
volatile acid  that  increases [$H^+$] through a series of reversible reactions
(Figure 3-6).

✔    Dissolved carbon dioxide and bicarbonate ions constitute most of a body
fluid's total carbon dioxide.

✔    All body fluid compartments are considered to be "open to the atmosphere"
for $CO_2$, because its reactions in solution are affected by [$CO_2$]$_{dissolved}$ (or
$PCO_2$).  $PCO_2$ in any fluid compartment is an independent variable set by the
balance between $CO_2$ production ($\dot{V}CO_2$) and its elimination by $\dot{V}_A$ .

✔ All reaction products of $CO_2$ in protein-free solutions (Figure 3-6) are dependent variables whose concentrations are determined by $PCO_2$ and [SID].

✔ Bicarbonate concentration is independent of $PCO_2$ in protein-free fluids where [SID] is positive. It is approximately equal to [SID]. $[H^+]$ is calculated by Equation 30.

✔ Dependent variables in any body fluid system are internal to the system and their values represent the system's reaction to the externally imposed values of the independent variables.

# Chapter 4

## Non-volatile Weak Acids

**What to Look for:**

In this chapter you will learn about:

- how proteins and phosphates in a body fluid influence its hydrogen ion concentration
- how plasma protein's net anionic charge is determined only by its albumin concentration and plasma pH; plasma globulins play no role
- how inorganic phosphate's ionic charge is determined by plasma pH and phosphate concentration
- "factor Z" and its relationship to the ionic concentration of dissolved phosphate

An aqueous solution is electrically neutral because, one way or another, electrical charges associated with all its anions equal that of all its cations. Some of these ions come from the dissociation of water itself and others come from strong ions that have been added to it, as described in

A "strong" molecule nearly completely dissociates into cations and anions in an aqueous solution. A "weak" molecule only incompletely dissociates. It contributes some ions to the solution, but also remains in its undissociated molecular form.

Chapter 2. Also, ions in biological fluids come from metabolically produced and dissolved carbon dioxide, as described in Chapter 3. Because carbon dioxide is effective as an acid and also appears in a gas phase as a normal constituent of alveolar gas, it is considered to be a "volatile acid". There are two other sources of ions in body fluids. They come from the non-volatile, weakly dissociated molecules of the different forms of inorganic phosphate and from proteins, as described in this chapter.

# Section A

## Dissociation of Weak Non-volatile Acids

All undissociated, non-volatile weak acids in body fluids are symbolized as "HA". Some are proteins, others are phosphates. They dissociate in an aqueous solution to contribute hydrogen ions ($H^+$) and anions ($A^-$), collectively symbolized as "$A^-$". That is:

$$[HA] \overset{K_A}{\rightleftharpoons} [H^+] + [A^-] \qquad (34)$$

and

$$K_A \cdot [HA] = [H^+] \cdot [A^-] \qquad (35)$$

The sum of [$A^-$] and [HA] is called "[$A_{TOT}$]". Because a solution's [$H^+$] depends, in part, on [$A^-$], the total concentration of non-volatile weak acids ([$A_{TOT}$]) consisting of both the undissociated ([HA]) and dissociated ([$A^-$]) forms must be evaluated.

The equation describing this conservation of mass, is:

$$[A_{TOT}] = [HA] + [A^-] \tag{36}$$

or

$$[HA] = [A_{TOT}] - [A^-] \tag{37}$$

By substitution of Equation 37 in Equation 35,

$$K_A \cdot ([A_{TOT}] - [A^-]) = [H^+] \cdot [A^-] \tag{38}$$

so that

$$[A^-] = \frac{K_A \cdot [A_{TOT}]}{K_A + [H^+]} \tag{39}$$

# Section B

## $[A_{TOT}]$ - The Third Independent Variable

Equation 25 (Chapter 3) described electrical neutrality in body fluids such as interstitial fluid and cerebrospinal fluid, which contain negligible concentrations of proteins. It did not account for anions contributed by the non-volatile weak acids. When these acids add $A^-$ to the solution, then:

$$[H^+] + [SID] - [OH^-] - [HCO_3^-] - [CO_3^{2-}] - [A^-] = 0 \tag{40}$$

To account for electrical neutrality in body fluids containing $CO_2$, strong ions and non-volatile weak acids, it is necessary to substitute Equation 39 for [A⁻] in Equation 40 and make appropriate substitutions for [OH⁻], [$HCO_3^-$] and [$CO_3^{2-}$], as in Equation 28, so that:

$$[H^+] + [SID] - \frac{K'_w}{[H^+]} - \frac{K_c \cdot PCO_2}{[H^+]} - \frac{K_3 \cdot K_c \cdot PCO_2}{[H^+]^2} - \frac{K_A \cdot [A_{TOT}]}{K_A + [H^+]} = 0 \qquad (41)$$

Multiplying both sides of Equation 41 by H² • ($K_A$ + [H⁺]) shows that:

$$
\begin{aligned}
[H^+]^4 &+ (K_A + [SID]) \cdot [H^+]^3 \\
&+ ((K_A \cdot ([SID] - [A_{TOT}])) - (K_c \cdot PCO_2 + K'_w)) \cdot [H^+]^2 \\
&- ((K_A \cdot (K_c \cdot PCO_2 + K'_w) + K_3 \cdot K_c \cdot PCO_2) \cdot [H^+] \\
&- K_A \cdot K_3 \cdot K_c \cdot PCO_2 = 0
\end{aligned}
\qquad (42)
$$

Equations 41 and 42 are important. They show that, in addition to the independent variables [SID] and $PCO_2$, the total concentration of non-volatile weak acids acts as an independent variable and affects [H⁺] and other dependent variables in solution. The analysis assumes a single, generic, weak, non-volatile acid with a single dissociation constant ($K_A$) representing the net effect produced by many dissociable groups (Stewart, 1981,1983; Fencl & Leith, 1993). The factor $K_A$ represents the combined effects of proteins and phosphates, as described later in this chapter (Sections C and D).

## B.1. Non-volatile Weak Acids in Plasma

Data in Figures 4-9 and 4-10 show that when [SID] is constant, plasma [H⁺] and [$HCO_3^-$] vary as functions of $PCO_2$, but both are influenced by [$A_{TOT}$]. When [$A_{TOT}$] is higher than normal, as would occur with a hyperalbuminemia, or hyper-

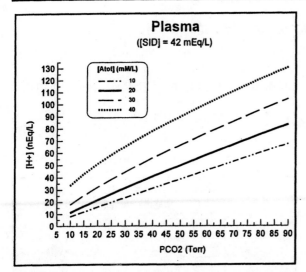

**Figure 4-9:** Hydrogen ion concentration in plasma varies as functions of $PCO_2$ and $[A_{TOT}]$ when [SID] is constant.

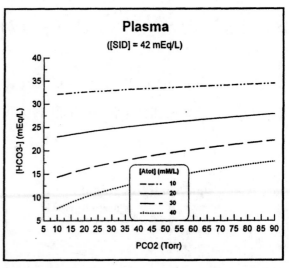

**Figure 4-10:** Bicarbonate ion concentration in plasma varies as functions of $PCO_2$ and $[A_{TOT}]$ when [SID] is constant.

phosphatemia, $[H^+]$ is also higher than normal, producing a non-respiratory acidemia. Implications of the relationships in Figure 4-9 explain recent observations (Rossing et.al., 1986; Figge et. al., 1991, 1992) that increasing albumin in plasma decreases its pH. This justifies albumin being considered an "acidic anion". When plasma albumin concentration falls, as with hemorrhage, pH increases because of a blood protein deficit. Hyperalbuminemia resulting from serum concentration contributes to the non-respiratory (so-called, "metabolic") acidosis associated with cholera (Wang et.al., 1986). Hypoalbuminemia is associated with liver cirrhosis and malnutrition (Rose & Post, 2001; Fencl & Leith, 1993) with a resulting non-respiratory ("metabolic") alkalosis.

Bicarbonate is a major anionic, dependent variable in plasma. When $[A_{TOT}]$ increases, $[A^-]$ also increases and $[HCO_3^-]$ decreases in order to maintain electrical neutrality, as shown in Figure 4-10. The reverse occurs when $[A_{TOT}]$ decreases.

## B.2. Non-volatile Weak Acids in Intracellular Fluid

Data in Figures 4-11 and 4-12 show the effects of $PCO_2$ and [SID] on [H+] and

[$HCO_3^-$] in intracellular fluid (ICF) when [$A_{TOT}$] is constant.  Both [$A_{TOT}$] and [SID]

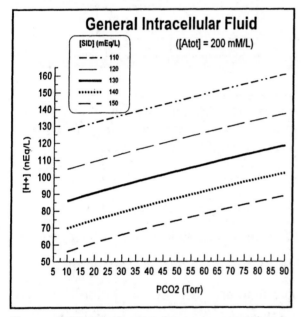

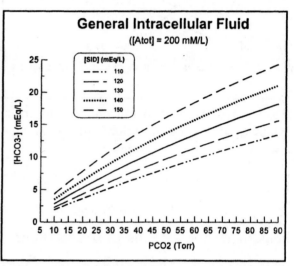

**Figure 4-11:** Hydrogen ion concentration in "general intracellular fluid" varies as functions of $PCO_2$ and [$A_{TOT}$] is constant.

**Figure 4-12:** Bicarbonate ion concentration in "general intracellular fluid" varies as functions of $PCO_2$ and [SID] when [$A_{TOT}$] is constant.

are higher in ICF than in plasma, as is [H+].  The ICF becomes more acidic as $PCO_2$ increases and [SID] decreases.  Bicarbonate concentration increases with increasing $PCO_2$ but less so when [SID] is low.

Cellular protein concentration is more stable than is that in plasma,  because of the impermeability of the cell membrane to large molecules.  Loss of either strong cations or anions from cells, however, is more likely to occur as a result of either osmotic or drug effects on metabolically driven ion pumps or ion channels.

Aqueous solutions containing strong ions, $CO_2$ and non-volatile weak acids have three independent variables (Stewart, 1978, 1983). As expressed in Equation 42, they are its strong ion difference (SID; Chapter 2), the partial pressure of its dissolved carbon dioxide ($PCO_2$; Chapter 3), and its total concentration of non-volatile weak acids ($A_{TOT}$). These factors set as dependent variables (Stewart, 1978) the solution's concentrations of hydrogen ions

> The electrical neutrality of an aqueous solution containing strong ions, carbon dioxide and non-volatile weak acids depends on three independent variables, $PCO_2$, [SID] and [$A_{TOT}$].

([$H^+$]), hydroxyl ions ([$OH^-$]), bicarbonate ions ([$HCO_3^-$]), carbonate ions ([$CO_3^{2-}$]), and the undissociated ([HA]) and dissociated ([$A^-$]) forms of the non-volatile weak acids. Equations 40 to 42 describe how these variables are related to one another in a steady state. Solution of Equation 42 for hydrogen ion concentration is straightforward, once data are available for the three independent variables and for the constants in the equation. When [$H^+$] is known, relationships among the other dependent variables are shown in Equation 41.

The factor,"$A_{TOT}$", in Equations 41 and 42 indicates the effects of all weakly dissociated, non-volatile acids in the solution. They are the different ionic forms of inorganic phosphate and the dissociable, exposed ionic groups of the amino acids found in proteins. The

> The effect of $A_{TOT}$ represents the combined influences of inorganic phosphate and proteins' amino acid anionic groups. Also, $K_A$ represents the net effect of their dissociation constants.

next two sections show how plasma pH influences the net effective valence of plasma inorganic phosphate and the dissociable groups in human serum albumin.

# Section C

# The Role of Proteins

Serum proteins play a major role in determining acid-base status. A protein is a polypeptide chain of amino acids joined by a peptide bond between the $\alpha$-amino group of one amino acid and the carboxyl group of another. Some amino acids have aromatic, imidazole, or sulfur-containing side groups and the protein chain has an amino terminus at one end and a carboxy terminus at the other. Some side groups determine the 3-dimensional structure of the protein itself. The side groups act as cationic (basic) or anionic (acidic) groups.

The amino acids lysine and arginine are cationic because their side chains are positively charged, but those for aspartic and glutamic acid are negatively charged. The net charge on a protein molecule is the algebraic sum of its oppositely charged side groups. Proteins affect the solution's [$H^+$], as do other electrically charged solutes. The effective pK or $K_A$ of a protein's unbound groups depends on how many there are, their proximity to others in the surrounding microenvironment, and the solution's [$H^+$] or pH (Reeves, 1997, Figge et. al., 1992 ).

The body's intracellular fluid compartments have the highest concentration of proteins. In muscle, for example, it is about 200 mEq/L (Stewart, 1981). Protein composition varies among different cells, but it is difficult to determine its effect on pH, because of the large differences in function among cells. For example, hemoglobin, the predominant intracellular protein in the red blood cell, increases the oxygen carrying capacity of blood because of four heme groups attached to the globin portion of the molecule.

Both [$H^+$] and $PCO_2$ of blood affect the ability of the heme to bind and release oxygen (West, 1995). The protein has thirty-eight histidine residues, each with an imidazole side group, which together have an effective pK close to normal blood pH. This provides a hydrogen ion binding site on the protein, which affects its 3-dimensional configuration and indirectly influences heme's ability to bind and release oxygen. Also, enzymatic activity is affected by [$H^+$], possibly because of heterogeneous distribution of microscopic pK's for specific histidine-imidazole groups (Reeves, 1976). Electrical charge may also be a force for holding charged metabolites inside a cell (Davis, 1958; Rahn , 1985). There are many reasons to consider that the preservation of protein charge state is the regulated variable in acid-base regulation (Reeves, 1997).

Blood plasma, has the highest concentration of proteins, compared to all other extracellular fluids. It contains primarily albumin (~60%; 4.5 g/dL) and globulins (~40%; 2.5 g/dL) (Guyton & Hall, 1996). There is normally little protein in interstitial fluid, because whatever leaks by bulk flow from damaged capillaries is soon cleared by lymphatic drainage.

The implication that plasma proteins are important for determining acid-base status was first made in 1928, based on the analysis of albumin and globulin fractions isolated from horse serum (Van Slyke et. al., 1928). Electrical charges carried by both molecules were shown to be linearly related to serum pH, although each had its own slope and consequently played its own role. They were described as having a net anionic charge of about 17 mEq/L at a pH of 7.4 and an albumin-to-globulin ratio of 1.6. Although the accuracy and precision of these measurements were later questioned (Van Leeuwen, 1964), these data were a landmark in understanding acid-base phenomena. It was such an important observation, that data for horse and human serum were considered to be the same for the next five decades. Even as late as 1981, the net anionic charge contributed by plasma protein was presented to be very nearly the same (16.6 mEq/L) as that published over fifty years earlier (Stewart, 1981).

The role of plasma protein in human serum is now considered to be quite different than it has been in the past. Serum globulin has been shown to have a negligible role in acid-base phenomena (Figge et. al., 1991, 1992) and the charge on plasma protein has been shown to be lower, about 12 mEq/L (Van Leeuwen, 1964; Figge, et. al., 1991).

There are several reasons to consider alternative analyses to define how the negative charges of protein and inorganic phosphate contribute to acid-base status. The acid-base state in biological fluids containing protein is determined by several independent variables, the strong ion difference ([SID]), the partial pressure of $CO_2$ ($PCO_2$) and the total concentration of non-volatile weak acids ([$A_{TOT}$]; Section B, Equation 42; Stewart, 1981,1983). The factor "$A_{TOT}$" in Equations 41 and 42 represents all non-volatile weak acids, such as proteins and inorganic phosphate, and assumes a single dissociation constant, $K_A$. The use of a single value for $K_A$ and $A_{TOT}$ (Stewart, 1981,1983), though, may be unjustified (Watson, 1999).

Calculations of pH using equation 42 do not agree well with measured pH, either in human patients (McAuliffe et al., 1986) or with measurements in human blood *in vitro* (Rossing et al., 1986). The problem is how to quantify the variations of concentrations of albumin and globulin with a single [$A_{TOT}$] (Figge et al., 1991). Also, the "Stewart model" (Stewart, 1981, 1983), which predicts how the negative charge on protein ([Pr⁻]; mEq/g) varies as a function of pH, requires reevaluation. Although it is reported to be a linear function (Van Slyke et al.,1928; Van Leeuwen, 1964; Siggaard-Andersen, 1974), it represents the simultaneous interaction of independently dissociating groups on the albumin and inorganic phosphate, and all with a single dissociation constant. A more complex model is required to account for the behavior of the weak non-volatile acids in serum.

## C.1. A New Mathematical Model

Plasma acid-base status has been reviewed so far (Equation 42) in respect to the effects of three independent variables, SID (the "strong ion difference"), $PCO_2$ and $A_{TOT}$ (the effect of non-volatile weak acids). This section considers two non-volatile weak acids which contribute independently to $A_{TOT}$, serum albumin (Alb) and inorganic phosphate ($P_i$; Figge

> This mathematical model requires considering two forms of $A_{TOT}$, one for albumin (Alb)and one for inorganic phosphate ($P_i$).

et al. 1991, 1992). The equation for electrical neutrality (Equation 40) is modified to reflect the separation of the single net negative charge on non-volatile weak acids ([A⁻]) into two separate anions, one for albumin ([Alb$^{x-}$]) and one for inorganic phosphate ([$P_i^{y-}$]) :

$$[H^+] + [SID] - [OH^-] - [HCO_3^-] - [CO_3^{2-}] - [Alb^{x-}] - [P_i^{y-}] = 0 \qquad (43)$$

The concentration of albumin has considerable influence on serum acid-base status. Some side groups of the albumin molecule are positively charged, some are negatively charged and some are electrically neutral over the normal range of plasma pH's (6.8-7.8). Their net effect, however, causes albumin to be an anion, but one with varying negative charge, depending on which side groups of the molecules are either binding, or releasing hydrogen ions. The imidazole group on the amino acid histidine, is the most influential. (Reeves, 1997; Watson, 1999).

Histidine plays an important, but complicated role in determining albumin's net electrical charge.  It is important, because its dissociation constant is within a normal range of pH for biological fluids.  It is complicated, because all of the 16 histidines  on the albumin molecule, have unique and different dissociation constants (Figge et al., 1992), possibly because of their different micro-environments.  Also, it is clear that some of the other side groups contributing both negative and positive charges remain unaltered with changes in hydrogen ion concentration, because their pK's are far removed from the normal range of biological fluid pH's (i.e. 6.8-7.8; Reeves, 1997, Watson, 1999).  Despite these complexities, however, there are still compelling reasons to consider the albumin molecule as independently contributing a net anionic charge.

A computer model (Figge et al., 1991, 1992)  evaluates  the contribution of each ionized, free portion of amino acids, whose net algebraic effect gives the albumin molecule its negative charge.  It also evaluates other factors in Equation 43.  The model, relevant to albumin, considered three factors: 1) data on the amino acid sequence of the albumin molecule , 2) the number of  ionizable side groups in the molecule (i.e. arginine, lysine, histidine, glutamic and aspartic acid, cysteine, tyrosine and the amino terminus and  carboxy  terminus), and 3) assigned dissociation constants to those groups.

For some side groups, known pK values were used for the chemical groups in proteins.  Also, for some, the number of ionizable  groups was less than the total number determined by amino acid sequence, because they were presumed to be buried in the protein molecule.  For others, the effective pK's were  unknown and had to be determined  by optimization methods using empirical data.  The albumin analysis was the most challenging segment of the program.

Serum inorganic phosphate  functions as a non-volatile weak acid and as an independent variable in determining pH. Its concentration is normally very low in plasma, so its decrease is unaccompanied by any change in acid-base status. It exists in three ionic forms in serum, $H_2PO_4^-$, $HPO_4^{2-}$ and to a lesser extent as $PO_4^{3-}$. Mono-hydrogen phosphate, with its bivalent negative charge is the most influential contributor in the biological range of pH from 6.8 to 7.8 (Sendroy & Hastings, 1927; Watson, 1999). The anionic contribution of phosphate ($[P_i^{y-}]$) was evaluated in addition to albumin and the other independent and dependent variables in Equation 43. In the computer model (Figge et. al, 1991, 1992) serum anionic phosphate ($[P_i^{y-}]$) was calculated as the product of inorganic phosphate concentration ($[P_i]$) and "factor Z" (see Section D.2.).

Mathematical analyses of the model (Figge et. al, 1991, 1992) show that pH ($\equiv \log 1/[H^+]$) of plasma or serum is set as a dependent variable because of the net interaction of four not three independent variables (Equation 42). Numerical iterative analyses isolate the independent effects in $[A_{TOT}]$ of albumin ($[Alb]$) and inorganic phosphate ($[P_i]$), so that:

$$pH = f_{pH} (PCO_2 , [SID] , [Alb] , [P_i] )$$ (44)

The validity of relationships in equation 44 was tested by a least squares statistic in which calculated pH ($pH_c$) using the model (Figge, et.al, 1991,1992) was compared to measured pH ($pH_m$) as:

$$S^2 = \Sigma (pH_c - pH_m )^2$$ (45)

The lower was $S^2$ , the more accurate was considered the evaluation of Equation

44  (Figge, et. al, 1991,1992).

The precision of relationships expressed in Equation 45 was tested in two kinds of solutions resembling human serum, one which contained only albumin, and one which contained both albumin and globulins.

## C.2. The New Mathematical Model: Results & Conclusions

Tests on the model showed that for human serum:

1)  All anionic charges on plasma proteins are on side groups of albumin, indicating that globulins have a negligible role in acid-base equilibria.

2)  For known values of the independent variables, [SID], $PCO_2$ and $[P_i]$, varying the concentration of albumin by itself affects pH and albumin's net negative charge ($[Alb^-]$).

3)  Confirmed by previous clinical findings (McAuliffe  et al., 1986) and *in vitro* studies (Rossing et al., 1986),  hypoproteinemia causes non-respiratory alkalosis and necessitates a downward adjustment of the anion gap (Gabow, 1985;Rose & Post, 2001).

4)  As confirmed *in vitro* studies (Rossing et al., 1986),  hyperproteinemia causes a non-respiratory acidosis. Also, the acidosis resulting from hemoconcentration in cholera (Wang et al., 1986) increases plasma [Alb] due to extracellular fluid volume depletion and also increases the anion gap (Rose & Post, 2001).

5) The ionized protein concentration ([Pr];mEq/g protein) is linearly related to pH, in the range 6.80-7.80, confirming data for albumin (Van Slyke et al., 1928; Van Leeuween, 1964 ).

6) [H$^+$], or pH, of plasma is a function of four independent variables, PCO$_2$, [SID], [P$_i$]and [Alb], and that all acid-base disturbances in plasma are a result of perturbations of any one or more of them.

7) A linear equation calculates ionized albumin ([Alb]) as a function of [Alb] and pH: If plasma albumin concentration and pH are known, the net negative charge on albumin is calculated as:

$$[Alb^{x-}] = 10 \cdot [Alb] \cdot (0.123 \cdot pH - 0.631) \qquad (46)$$

where:

$[Alb^{x-}]$ = net negative charge displayed by albumin (mEq/L)

[Alb] = albumin concentration (g/dL)

# Section D

## The Role of Inorganic Phosphate

This section describes how the effects of a solution's total concentration of inorganic phosphate ([P$_i$]$_{TOT}$) operate through the factor of "A$_{TOT}$". Both ([P$_i$]$_{TOT}$) and plasma pH determine the effective valence, ([P$_i^{x}$]). The phosphate effect is through [A$^-$], as shown in Equation 40.

## D.1. Determinants of Plasma Phosphate Concentration

The effect of a reduced concentration of inorganic phosphate on the acid-base status of plasma is small, because of its normally low concentration (2.5-4.5 mg/dL; 0.8-1.5 mmol/L). Hypophosphatemia, for example, has little effect on acid-base status. Hyperphosphatemia, however, contributes to the development of a non-respiratory ("metabolic") acidemia (Fencl & Leith, 1993).

Blood plasma is the most commonly used body fluid to evaluate $[P_i]_{TOT}$ clinically. It is easily collected and is a useful clinical reference. Intracellular $[P_i]$ varies among tissues, and also within a tissue. For example, magnetic resonance imaging (MRI) shows that $[P_i]$ is not only different for "fast twitch" and "slow twitch" muscles, but it also varies with their contractile state (Adams et. al., 1990).

Inorganic phosphate is readily absorbed by the gastrointestinal tract from milk, meat, fish and poultry products, which are its main dietary sources. The recommended dietary allowance for phosphorus is 800-1200 mg/day. How much is absorbed depends on its concentration in ingested food. When

> Inorganic phosphate concentration ($[P_i]$) is routinely measured for plasma to provide clinically useful information. Intracellular $[P_i]$ is more variable among cells and it is more difficult to sample.

dietary levels of phosphorus are low (less than 2 mg/(kg BW·day)), about 80-90% is absorbed. When it is high (more than 10 mg/(kg BW·day)), about 70% is absorbed. About 85% of the body's phosphorus is sequestered in the skeleton as $Ca_3(PO_4)_2$. Because of inorganic phosphate's close association with calcium ion, parathyroid hormone (PTH) plays a role in the regulation of both ionic concentrations in plasma (Rose & Post, 2001; Holick et. al., 1987).

The body's inorganic phosphate, [$P_i$], is closely controlled through renal function, but more in relation to [$Ca^{2+}$], than it is to acid-base status. Normally 80-95% of the filtered $P_i$ ("filtered load") is reabsorbed in the proximal renal tubules. At normal plasma pH (about 7.4), the filtered $P_i$ is predominantly in the form $HPO_4^{2-}$. It moves from the lumen into the cell by a specific $2Na^+:1HPO_4^{2-}$ stoichiometry transporter in the luminal membrane, which is regulated by both plasma [$P_i$] and PTH. As tubular fluid becomes more acidic, most of the $P_i$ is converted to $H_2PO_4^-$. The amount of $H^+$ bound by phosphate in renal tubular fluid is measured as titratable acid (Rose & Post, 2001). Renal reabsorption of phosphate depends on Na reabsorption. Sodium ions not absorbed by the proximal tubule may be absorbed distally, but $P_i$ will not be, so that the effects of a volume expansion and decreased Na reabsorption are to increase phosphate clearance (Holick et al., 1987).

Acute hyperphosphatemia is asymptomatic, but when chronic, it produces $Ca_3(PO_4)_2$ deposits. It is associated with hypoparathyroidism,

> Although a short-term increase in blood phosphate levels is innocuous, it is more serious when longstanding.

causing increased renal tubular reabsorption, hyperthyroidism, chronic renal failure, extensive cellular and tissue damage, and increased release of phosphate from muscle secondary to renal failure (Potts, 1987; Rose & Post, 2001). Intracellular phosphate depletion with an initially elevated plasma [$PO_4$] is common in diabetic ketoacidosis and non-ketonic hyperglycemia. Loss of $PO_4$, though, is primarily because of decreased dietary intake and increased urinary losses resulting from osmotic diuresis, the direct effect of acidemia and the rise in plasma [$PO_4$]. This hyperphosphatemia is readily corrected with insulin therapy (Rose & Post, 2001).

## D.2. Determining Ionized Phosphate Concentration

Dissolved phosphate ion has three forms which have valences from one to three. Phosphoric acid is a very strong acid (pK@37°C = 1.91). It dissociates in solution into three ionic forms, releasing a hydrogen ion at each step.

$$H_3PO_4 \rightleftharpoons^{①} H^+ + H_2PO_4^- \rightleftharpoons^{②} H^+ + HPO_4^{2-} \rightleftharpoons^{③} H^+ + PO_4^{3-} \qquad (47)$$

Reaction ①: $K_A$ = 1.22 •$10^{-2}$ mol/L (p$K_A$ = 1.91) ; reaction ②: $K_A$ = 2.19 •$10^{-7}$ mol/L (p$K_A$= 6.66) ; reaction ③: $K_A$ = 1.66 • $10^{-12}$ mol/L (p$K_A$ = 11.78); all at 37°C (Figge et. al.,1991; Sendroy & Hastings, 1927).

The amount of inorganic phosphate $[P_i^-]$ (mEq/L) which contributes charges to the electrical neutrality equation for plasma, is measured by the total phosphate concentration ($[P_i]$) and either the pH or $[H^+]$ of the solution.

Because of the Law of Mass Action, for the reactions in Equation 47,

$$K_1 = \frac{[H^+] \cdot [H_2PO_4^-]}{[H_3PO_4]} \qquad K_2 = \frac{[H^+] \cdot [HPO_4^{2-}]}{[H_2PO_4^-]} \qquad K_3 = \frac{[H^+] \cdot [PO_4^{3-}]}{[HPO_4^{2-}]}$$

The mass balance equation for phosphates is:

$$[P_i] = [H_3PO_4] + [H_2PO_4^-] + [HPO_4^{2-}] + [PO_4^{3-}] \qquad (48)$$

where , $[P_i]$ = total concentration of phosphate (mmol/L)

To define the influence of either $[H^+]$, or pH on phosphate ionization, (the so-called "factor Z";Figge et. al., 1991, 1992):

1) Make appropriate substitutions in Equation 48, expressing all forms of phosphate as functions of $[H_3PO_4]$ :

$$[P_i] = [H_3PO_4] + \frac{K_1 \cdot [H_3PO_4]}{[H^+]} + \frac{K_1 \cdot K_2 \cdot [H_3PO_4]}{[H^+]^2} + \frac{K_1 \cdot K_2 \cdot K_3 \cdot [H_3PO_4]}{[H^+]^3} \qquad (49)$$

2) Multiply both sides of equation 49 by $[H^+]^3$ :

$$[P_i] \cdot [H^3] = [H_3PO_4] \cdot [H^+]^3 + [H_3PO_4] \cdot K_1 \cdot [H^+]^2$$
$$+ [H_3PO_4] \cdot K_1 \cdot K_2 \cdot [H^+] + [H_3PO_4] \cdot K_1 \cdot K_2 \cdot K_3 \qquad (50)$$

3) Solve for $[H_3PO_4]$ :

$$[H_3PO_4] = [P_i] \cdot \frac{[H^+]^3}{[H^+]^3 + K_1 \cdot [H^+]^2 + K_1 \cdot K_2 \cdot [H^+] + K_1 \cdot K_2 \cdot K_3} \qquad (51)$$

4) Make appropriate substitutions in Equation 48, expressing all forms of phosphate as functions of $[H_2PO_4^-]$ :

$$[P_i] = \frac{[H^+] \cdot [H_2PO_4^-]}{K_1} + [H_2PO_4^-] + \frac{K_2 \cdot [H_2PO_4^-]}{[H^+]} + \frac{K_2 \cdot K_3 \cdot [H_2PO_4^-]}{[H^+]^2} \qquad (52)$$

5) Similar to steps 2 & 3, multiply both sides of Equation 52 by $(K_1 \cdot [H^+]^2)$, then solve for $[H_2PO_4^-]$ :

$$[H_2PO_4^-] = [P_i] \cdot \frac{K_1 \cdot [H^+]^2}{[H^+]^3 + K_1 \cdot [H^+]^2 + K_1 \cdot K_2 \cdot [H^+] + K_1 \cdot K_2 \cdot K_3} \qquad (53)$$

6) Make appropriate substitutions in Equation 48, expressing all forms of phosphate as functions of $[HPO_4^{2-}]$ :

$$[P_i] = \frac{[H^+]^2 \cdot [HPO_4^{2-}]}{K_1 \cdot K_2} + \frac{[H^+] \cdot [HPO_4^{2-}]}{K_2} + [HPO_4^{2-}] + \frac{K_3 \cdot [HPO_4^{2-}]}{[H^+]} \qquad (54)$$

7) Similar to steps 2 & 3, multiply both sides of Equation 54 by $(K_1 \cdot K_2 \cdot [H^+])$, then solve for $[HPO_4^{2-}]$ :

$$[HPO_4^{2-}] = [P_i] \cdot \frac{K_1 \cdot K_2 \cdot [H^+]}{[H^+]^3 + K_1 \cdot [H^+]^2 + K_1 \cdot K_2 \cdot [H^+] + K_1 \cdot K_2 \cdot K_3} \qquad (55)$$

8) Make appropriate substitutions in Equation 48, expressing all forms of phosphate as functions of $[PO_4^{3-}]$ :

$$[P_i] = \frac{[PO_4^{3-}] \cdot [H^+]^3}{K_1 \cdot K_2 \cdot K_3} + \frac{[PO_4^{3-}] \cdot [H^+]^2}{K_2 \cdot K_3} + \frac{[PO_4^{3-}] \cdot [H^+]}{K_3} + [PO_4^{3-}] \qquad (56)$$

9) Similar to steps 2 & 3, multiply both sides of Equation 56 by $(K_1 \cdot K_2 \cdot K_3)$, then solve for $[PO_4^{3-}]$ :

$$[PO_4^{3-}] = [P_i] \cdot \frac{K_1 \cdot K_2 \cdot K_3}{[H^+]^3 + K_1 \cdot [H^+]^2 + K_1 \cdot K_2 \cdot [H^+] + K_1 \cdot K_2 \cdot K_3} \qquad (57)$$

10) To change concentrations to equivalents of negative charge, multiply each phosphate species in the mass balance equation (Equation 48) by its charge, then sum the terms:

$$[P_i] = 0 \cdot [H_3PO_4] + 1 \cdot [H_2PO_4^-] + 2 \cdot [HPO_4^{2-}] + 3 \cdot [PO_4^{3-}] \qquad (58)$$

11) All expressions in denominators for Equations 51, 53, 55 & 57, are the same, so terms in the numerator are summed. Since $H_3PO_4$ (Equation 58) has no charge, it is eliminated from the final solution:

$$Z = \frac{K_1 \cdot [H^+]^2 + 2 \cdot K_1 \cdot K_2 \cdot [H^+] + 3 \cdot K_1 \cdot K_2 \cdot K_3}{[H^+]^3 + K_1 \cdot [H^+]^2 + K_1 \cdot K_2 \cdot [H^+] + K_1 \cdot K_2 \cdot K_3} \qquad (59)$$

12) Then $Z \bullet [P_i]$ (mmol/L) = the concentration ($[P_i^{y-}]$) in mEq/L (Figge et. al., 1991).

When pH = 7.40, Z = 1.85, indicating that the inorganic phosphate exists mainly as $HPO_4^{2-}$ and $H_2PO_4^-$ . For pH's 6.90 to 7.8, Z varies from 1.64 to 1.93. When pH = 7.40, and $[P_i]$ is low (2.5 mg/dL; 0.8 mmol/L), ionic phosphate $[P_i^{y-}]$ = 1.5 mEq/L. With hyperphosphatemia (i.e. $[P_i]$ = 7.5 mg/dL; 2.4 mmol/L), $[P_i^{y-}]$ = 4.4

mEq/L. The anionic charges contributed by inorganic phosphate are a function of both total phosphate concentration and pH of the solution.

If plasma pH and total phosphate concentration ($[P_i]$) are measured, ionized phosphate ( $[P_i^{\,y-}]$) is a linear function described by (Figge et. al.,1992):

$$[P_i^-] = [P_i] \cdot (0.309 \cdot pH - 0.469) \qquad (60)$$

where:

$[P_i]$ is in units of mmol/L

Measurements of plasma total phosphate ($[P_i]$) are typically reported in units of mg/dL of phosphorus. To convert from mg/dL to mmol/L, multiply the measured value by 10/30.97; 10 converts to mg/L and 30.97 is the gram atomic weight of phosphorus.

# Section E

## Main Points from Chapter 4

✔    Non-volatile weak acids, inorganic phosphate and proteins represent a third independent variable in biological fluids, in addition to [SID] and $PCO_2$.

✔    In the "Stewart model" of acid-base balance, the total concentration of non-volatile weak acids ($[A_{TOT}]$) is the third independent variable with a single dissociation constant, $K_A$.   [H+] is calculated by Equation 42.

✔    The *Law of Conservation of Mass* applied to the non-volatile weak acids requires that the total concentration of the acid  ($[A_{TOT}]$) is equal to the sum of the concentrations of  undissociated acid ([HA]) and the dissociated form ($[A^-]$).

✔    A new model for non-volatile weak acids (Figge et. al., 1991,1992) considers  $[A_{TOT}]$ as two separate entities in serum, one representing albumin ([Alb]) and the other representing inorganic phosphate ($[P_i]$).

✔    All acid-base disturbances causing changes in the dependent variable, plasma pH ($\equiv \log 1/[H^+]$), are due to perturbations in plasma [SID], $PCO_2$, [Alb] and $[P_i]$, or combinations of these four independent variables.  To evaluate whole body acid-base status, based on blood plasma composition, it is necessary to evaluate quantitatively all four of these independent variables.

✔ The concentration of ionic albumin ($[Alb^{x-}]$) is a linear function of plasma [Alb] and pH. Equation 46 calculates $[Alb^{x-}]$.

✔ The concentration of ionic inorganic phosphate ($[P_i^{y-}]$) is a linear function of plasma $[P_i]$ and pH. Equation 60 calculates $[P_i^{y-}]$.

# Chapter 5

## Composition of Body Fluids

**What to Look for:**

In this chapter you will learn about:

- how independent variables determine body fluid composition
- the application of the law of electrical neutrality to body solutions
- the application of "gamblegrams" to body fluid composition
- why $[HCO_3^-]$ equals [SID] in interstitial fluid
- why hydrogen ion concentration in gastric juice is high
- why bicarbonate ion concentration in pancreatic juice is high
- why the concentration of dependent variables in body solutions can not be explained by either their active transport or exchange with strong ions

This chapter applies HION concepts to the analyses of three body fluids, interstitial fluid, blood plasma and intracellular fluid (Figure 1-2 and Table 1-2) which together comprise about 95% of all the body's aqueous solutions, yet vary widely among themselves in their molecular and ionic concentrations and in how they are formed. Analyses of plasma are commonly used clinically to reflect acid-base status and hydration, as well as to reveal respiratory and non-respiratory ("metabolic") compensations to physiological stressors. More commonly used analyses, like the gaseous and electrolyte composition of plasma, for example, are considered to index "whole body" acid-base status, not that of individual fluid compartments. This chapter also describes how gastric juice and pancreatic juice are formed and presents how their compositions depend on their strong ion difference ([SID]).

To understand HION principles and the explanations based on them for how aqueous fluids become either acidic or basic, it is necessary to distinguish between those dissolved ions which function as dependent variables, and those which operate as independent variables.  In all biological fluids, [SID], [$A_{TOT}$] and $PCO_2$ are exclusively independent variables.   This means

> Biological fluids establish their pH in response to environmental and metabolic circumstances brought to bear by the independent variables, [SID], [$A_{TOT}$] and $PCO_2$

that whatever external environmental and biological phenomena set them, they subsequently obligate the concentration of the fluid's dependent variables [$H^+$], [$OH^-$], [$HCO_3^-$], [$CO_3^{2-}$], [HA], and [$A^-$].  The profile of the fluid's dependent variables, is an obligatory consequence of the physical chemical relationships among themselves in reversible chemical reactions, all depending on, and driven by, the solution's [SID], [$A_{TOT}$] and $PCO_2$. This is how gastric juice becomes acidic (Section B.1.) and how pancreatic juice becomes characteristically  basic (Section B.2.).  It is also how any other body fluid establishes its pH.

In an aqueous solution containing only strong ions, the constraints of water dissociation equilibrium and electrical neutrality require that [$H^+$] and [$OH^-$] assume specific values as soon as the independent variable, [SID], has been set  (Equations 15 and 16).  If the solution is exposed to carbon dioxide, there are even more constraints because of the independent variable, $PCO_2$.  Bicarbonate and carbonate

(Equations 22 and 23), in addition to the water dissociation equilibrium defining $[H^+]$ and $[OH^-]$, are now affected by $PCO_2$. Equation 25 shows these relationships and allows for the calculation of $[H^+]$ (Equation 29).

Hydrogen ion is the common link in all the descriptions of incomplete dissociation reactions of the other dependent variables' concentrations and provides a means for deriving their concentration values. Blood plasma and intracellular fluid have more constraints because of their weak, non-volatile acids, treated as a lumped parameter ($[A_{TOT}]$), which exist in both undissociated ($[HA]$) and dissociated ($[A^-]$) forms. The equation for electrical neutrality (Equation 40) requires accounting for

> Hydrogen ion is the common factor for relationships among dependent variables in a biological fluid.

the ionic form (Equation 39), in addition to the other dependent variables previously considered. The solution for $[H^+]$ is reflected in a more complex fourth-order equation (Equation 42). Plasma $[A_{TOT}]$ has an ionic component from plasma albumin ($[Alb^{x-}]$ ;Equation 46) and another from inorganic phosphate ($[P_i^{y-}]$; Equation 60).

In body fluids without significant protein concentrations, such as interstitial fluid, cerebrospinal fluid, gastric juice and pancreatic juice, Equation 29 indicates that $[H^+]$ is determined by 2 independent variables, $[SID]$ and $PCO_2$. It also represents the simultaneous solution of four independent equations (i.e. those for water dissociation, bicarbonate formation, carbonate formation and the equation for electrical neutrality).

# Section A

## The Body Fluid Compartments

### A.1. Interstitial Fluid

This chapter presents a graphical method, the "gamblegram" (Figs. 5-13, 5-14, 5-15, 5-16, 5-19) to show  the distribution of ions in body fluid compartments (Gamble, 1952;  Harvey, 1979).  It uses two bars, one to show the proportional concentrations of cations and another to show the proportional concentrations of anions.  The gamblegram documents  well the relationship that any aqueous solution, including body fluids, must conform to the Law of Electrical Neutrality. That is, the sum of all cations must equal that of all anions.  This is shown by  the equal heights of the two bars in a gamblegram.

Figure 5-13  expresses, for example, the fundamentally important relationship that the total concentration of cations equals that of anions because both bars have equal height.  This is about 143 mEq/L for interstitial fluid.  The recognition that total anionic and cationic concentrations are equal in any body fluid is, by definition, the "Law of Electrical Neutrality" for  these solutions.   It underlies the central principle expressed for water (Chapter 2, Equation 7), for an aqueous solution with dissolved strong ions (Chapter 2, Equation 10), and specifically for interstitial fluid (Chapter 3, Equation 25).

The relative concentrations of whatever anionic and cationic species constitute the total in each group varies widely and is unique for each body fluid.  The totals, however, for all cations and for all anions must be equal, no matter what ionic profile any specific solution has, because all aqueous solutions are electrically neutral.

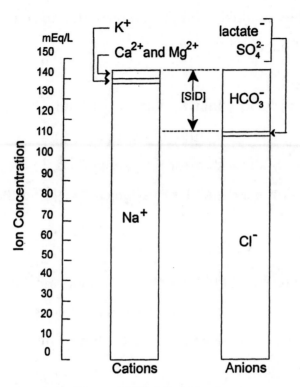

**Figure 5-13** Interstitial fluid ionic composition

Data in Figure 5-13 show that sodium ions predominate as a cation in interstitial fluid. Other strong cations (i.e., those with $K > 10^{-4}$ Eq/L; pK < 4) in this solution are potassium, calcium and magnesium (Chapter 2, Section C.1.). Chloride, lactate and sulfate are the strong anions in this body fluid. Bicarbonate is the predominant weak anion,

> Sodium ion is the predominant strong cation in interstitial fluid. Chloride is the predominant strong anion. Bicarbonate is the predominant weak anion.

because interstitial fluid, like all other body fluids, reflects the influence of carbon dioxide. This metabolically produced gas reacts with water to form carbonic acid, whose major dissociation product is bicarbonate (Figure 3-6). The contributions of the dependent variables of hydrogen, hydroxyl and carbonate ions are not represented in Figure 5-13, because of their low concentrations. The difference between the concentration of strong cations and strong anions in interstitial fluid, as it is for any other aqueous fluid, is expressed as "the strong ion difference" ([SID]; see: Chapter 2, Section C.2.).

Data in Figure 5-13 also show that for interstitial fluid, the concentration of bicarbonate ions is equal to [SID], confirming data in Figure 3-8. Also, data in Figure 3-7 and Equation 29 show that for interstitial fluid, hydrogen ion concentration depends on the independent variables [SID] and the partial pressure of carbon dioxide.

[SID] is positive for interstitial fluid, as shown in Figure 5-13. This is because there is a predominance of strong cations over strong anions in the solution, even though the concentration of all cations is equal to that of all anions. The larger that [SID] is positive, the lower is the concentration of hydrogen ions in the solution, and the more alkaline is the solution. The reverse is also true. When [SID] is negative in an aqueous solution, because the concentration of strong anions is larger than that of

> The larger that [SID] is positive in an aqueous solution, the lower is $[H^+]$ in the solution, and the more alkaline is the solution. The larger that [SID] is negative in an aqueous solution, the greater is $[H^+]$ and the more acidic is the solution.

strong cations, the greater is the concentration of hydrogen ions, and the more acid is the solution (Chapter 2, Section C.3. and Figure 2-5). This effect is described for gastric juice in Section B.1.

Although the concept of [SID] had not been expressed when gamblegrams were first published (Gamble et. al., 1923), its importance was, nonetheless, recognized, even at the time. Strong cations were called "bases", because when they were added to a solution, their net effect was to reduce its hydrogen ion concentration.

Also, sodium, potassium, magnesium and calcium ions were considered to be "fixed", implying their persistence (because of their high dissociation constants) in an ionic state as "strong ions".

> Evaluating a solution's [SID] is a more direct way to understand the ionic mechanisms, which determine its acid-base status.

Similarly, because the net effect of increasing a solution's concentration of strong anions increased hydrogen ion concentration, they were called "acids". These effects are expressed contemporarily in terms of changing [SID]. Equating the change in an aqueous solution's hydrogen ion concentration to differences in its electrically charged strong anions and cations (i.e., [SID]) is simpler, more rational and easier to defend, than it is to consider this phenomenon on the basis of the Bronsted-Lowry definition (Cohen & Kassirer, 1982; Fencl-Leith, 1993), which considers that an acid is a "proton donor" and that a base is a "proton acceptor".

## A.2. Blood Plasma

Blood plasma, like interstitial fluid, is an extracellular fluid compartment (see Figure 1-2). It is the body fluid that is most frequently analyzed clinically, because samples are easily collected and its composition gives important diagnostic information. Techniques for analyzing blood plasma and concepts for interpreting results to determine "whole body" acid-base status, which are still used today, were developed at the beginning of the twentieth century. Basic relationships among plasma hydrogen ion concentration, bicarbonate ion concentration and the partial pressure of carbon dioxide are commonly expressed using the often-referenced Henderson-Hasselbalch equation:

$$pH = pK' + Log\left(\frac{[HCO_3^-]}{\alpha \cdot PCO_2}\right) \qquad (61)$$

Equation 61 is a valid expression for some biological fluids, but not for all of them. It is accurately applicable to interstitial fluid (Figure 5-13), for example, because its bicarbonate ion concentration does not vary as a function of the partial pressure of carbon dioxide (Figure 3-8), but it does vary as a function of [SID]. Data in Figures 3-8 and 5-13 show, in fact, that [$HCO_3^-$] ([Total $CO_2$]) for interstitial fluid is equal to [SID]. This is because interstitial fluid does not contain non-volatile weak acids, as do blood plasma and intracellular fluids. For interstitial fluid, Equation 61 can be accurately expressed in a form similar to Equation 33, as:

$$pH = pK_c + Log\left(\frac{[SID]}{\alpha \cdot PCO_2}\right) \qquad (62)$$

In body fluids containing significant concentrations of weak non-volatile acids (i.e. proteins and inorganic phosphates), such as plasma and intracellular fluid, Equation 42 shows a lumped parameter, [$A_{TOT}$], a third independent variable in addition to [SID] and $PCO_2$ , which determine the concentrations of the dependent variables (i.e. [$H^+$], [$OH^-$], [$HCO_3^-$], [$CO_3^{2-}$], [HA] and [$A^-$]). The concentration of $A^-$ depends on the sum of ionized albumin (Equation 46) and on

Traditional Henderson-Hasselbalch analyses are useful for only a first-order evaluation of a biological solution's acid-base status. They are intrinsically incomplete and fail to express important relationships between the fluid's independent and dependent variables.

ionized phosphate (Equation 60) in plasma. Relationships expressed in Equation 61 are incomplete from dependent variables. That is, it does not show what is changing physiologically (independent variables) and what happens because of it (dependent variables). Also it does not recognize that $HCO_3^-$ is itself, like $H^+$(pH), a dependent variable whose concentration is set by the independent variables, $PCO_2$,

[SID], [Alb] and [P$_i$].  This misuse of the Henderson-Hasselbalch equation has

caused numerous investigators over many years to consider incorrectly that [H$^+$]

and [HCO$_3^-$] are independent variables, comparable to [SID] and PCO$_2$, rather than

recognize them more accurately as dependent variables in obligatory, reversible

chemical reactions.


The ionic composition of blood plasma  represented as a gamblegram is shown

in Figure 5-14.

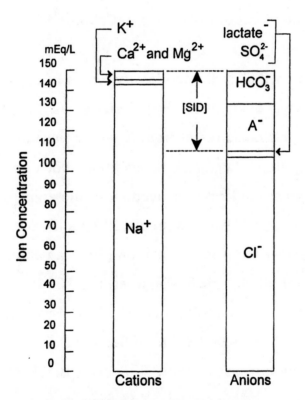

**Figure 5-14** Plasma ionic composition.
Lactate and sulfate are strong anions.
The ionic forms of albumin (Alb$^-$) and
phosphate (P$_i$) are shown as A$^-$.

As for Figure 5-13 (the gamblegram for interstitial fluid), the electrical neutrality of

blood plasma is established by equal concentrations of cations and anions of about

150 mEq/L . Cationic composition for blood plasma is the same as for interstitial fluid. Anionic composition, however, is different. Weak anions are not only [$HCO_3^-$] ([Total $CO_2$]), but also the anionic form of the non-volatile weak acids (albumin and inorganic phosphate) in plasma, symbolized in Figure 5-14 as, "$A^-$". Although [SID] is positive and approximately the same as for interstitial fluid, total weak anions for plasma are the balanced, reciprocal relationship between [$A^-$] and [$HCO_3^-$]. As expressed in Equation 36, the total concentration of non-volatile weak acids, [$A_{TOT}$], includes the undissociated (HA) and the dissociated ($A^-$) forms. The dissociated form of albumin ([$Alb^{x-}$]) and inorganic phosphate ([$P_i^{y-}$]) are calculated using Equation 46 and Equation 60, respectively (Chapter 4, Sections C & D).

Blood plasma is often used clinically to identify whole body acid-base status. If its total osmolarity remains constant, its [$H^+$] increases as [SID] becomes less positive and *vice versa*. This could result from a net increase in its strong anions (chloride, lactate, sulfate, etc.). Acidemia, for example, could result from hyperchloremia, or an increase in lactate caused by tissue anoxia, or related to the effects of exercise. Similarly, alkalemia is produced by a hypochloremia, causing an increase in [SID], or a decrease in [$Alb^{x-}$], resulting from a decrease in [Alb], hypoalbuminemia ( Rossing et. al., 1986; Figge et. al., 1991) possibly from starvation, or liver disease. Their net effect is to reduce [$H^+$]. As shown later, any decrease in plasma [SID] will increase [$H^+$] (See Section B.2.3. and Table 5-6) and an increase in plasma [SID] decreases [$H^+$] (See Section B.1.3. and Table 5-4).

### A.3. Intracellular Fluid

Figure 5-15 is a gamblegram showing ionic composition for intracellular fluid. Although cationic composition is the same as for interstitial fluid (Figure 5-13) and for blood plasma (Figure 5-14), it is different for intracellular fluid in which potassium ions predominate.

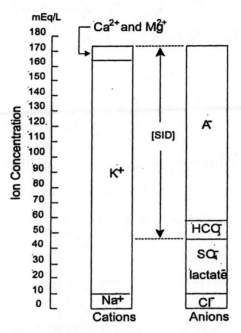

**Figure 5-15** General Intracellular Fluid ionic composition. Ionized weak non-volatile acids are shown as A⁻.

Similarly, chloride ions are in the highest concentration as the strong anion in interstitial fluid and plasma, but they aren't for intracellular fluid. Also, in contrast to blood plasma, $A^-$ is the predominant weakly dissociated ion in intracellular fluid. Intracellular fluid

> Potassium ions predominate as the strong cation in intracellular fluid, but chloride ions are not its most concentrated anion.

(ICF) contains non-volatile weak acids, as does plasma, but the proteins in ICF are more variable among cells and organs and their role in acid-base regulation is not known. Until better definition of intracellular protein composition is available, a lumped parameter model ($[A_{TOT}]$), as in Equation 42, best estimates ICF's dependent variable concentrations. Although all body fluids show the influence of [SID], it is the greatest in intracellular fluid, because strong anions, such as chloride, are comparatively less abundant.

### A.4. What It All Means

Because interstitial fluid (Figure 5-13) does not contain non-volatile weak acids, its [H$^+$] is set by only four factors. Equation 6 describes the reversible effects of the dissociation of water. Equation 22 describes the formation of bicarbonate. Equation 23 shows the formation of carbonate from bicarbonate, and Equation 25 incorporates relationships in Equations 6, 22 and 23 with [SID] in establishing electrical neutrality. The common link among these interactions is the dependent

> Unlike blood plasma and intracellular fluid, interstitial fluid does not contain non-volatile weak acids, which require evaluating the effects of [A$_{TOT}$].

variable, [H$^+$]. The composition of interstitial fluid involves two of the three independent variables affecting any body fluid's acid-base status, [SID] and PCO$_2$, as shown in Equation 29. When [H$^+$] in interstitial fluid is known, values for [OH$^-$], [HCO$_3^-$] and [CO$_3^{2-}$] are calculated using relationships for each in Equation 28.

It is unnecessary to evaluate the effects of [A$_{TOT}$] and [A$^-$],for interstitial fluid because it does not contain non-volatile weak acids, as do blood plasma and intracellular fluid. For them, two additional relationships must be considered. Equation 35 describes the dissociation of HA into H$^+$ and A$^-$. Equation 36 describes the "Conservation of Mass" for non-volatile weak acids related to the undissociated form (HA) and the dissociated form (A$^-$), collectively represented as [A$_{TOT}$]. Equation

40 expresses relationships of electrical neutrality similar to Equation 25, but it includes solutions of Equations 35 and 37, which show the effect of $[A^-]$. Equation 42 calculates $[H^+]$ showing the effects of $[SID]$, $[A_{TOT}]$ and $PCO_2$ as independent variables in a less well defined fluid, such as intracellular fluid.

In plasma, albumin concentration ($[Alb]$) and inorganic phosphate concentration ($[P_i]$), in addition to $[SID]$ and $PCO_2$, represent four independent variables, which define more completely the dependent variable concentrations in this fluid. Hydrogen ion is the common link for all equations for dependent variables. Henderson-Hasselbalch analyses (Equation 61) consider only those factors expressed in Equation 22. Such an analysis falls far short of describing how ionic composition is formulated for fluids containing non-volatile weak acids, like blood plasma.

# Section B

## Secreted Fluids

The major function of the gastrointestinal tract is to digest and absorb nutrients from ingested food. This involves breaking down complex proteins, fats and carbohydrates into smaller molecules for absorption by the small intestine and distribution by the blood to body tissues for use in metabolic processes. An important step in this complex process is to mix the contents of the gastrointestinal tract with secreted fluids at different stages in the digestive sequence. The total volume of fluid secreted by the body to facilitate digestion is large. In humans, for example, salivary glands, glandular tissue in the stomach, pancreas, liver and small intestine secrete six to seven liters of fluid each day into the lumen of the gastrointestinal tract (Guyton & Hall, 1996).

Not only is there a large volume of secreted fluids, but also, they have considerably different hydrogen ion concentrations at different places in the gut. The upper gastrointestinal tract, for example, is acid. Although the pH of saliva from unstimulated glands is only 6.0 to 7.0, that for gastric juice is strongly acidic, with a pH range from 0.8 to 3.0 (Guyton & Hall,1996; Davenport, 1977). The luminal contents of the lower gastrointestinal tract beginning at the duodenum are alkaline, largely because of pancreatic secretions whose pH is from 7.6 to 8.3 (Davenport, 1977; Guyton & Hall,1996).

Physiologists have investigated and evaluated for a long time the processes which underlie the normal and characteristically large range of acidity in the gut. There have been many, often elaborate, explanations. Those which include HION concepts, though, are relatively simple and easily fit long

| |
|---|
| Gastric juice is highly acidic and pancreatic juice is strongly basic. They represent extremes of pH for biologically secreted fluids. Their normal physiologic functions depend heavily on these unique acid-base properties. |

established observations about gastrointestinal environments. They explain not only how pH is established, but also how gastric and pancreatic secretions are formed, as described in the following sections.

## B.1. Gastric Juice

### B.1.1. Traditional Concepts of Gastric Juice Formation

It is often supposed that the

| |
|---|
| Contrary to claims in many textbooks, gastric juice does not contain hydrochloric acid (HCl), but it is, nonetheless, strongly acidic. HION concepts show how all this comes about. |

stomach contains hydrochloric acid (HCl), because of the secretion of gastric juice
( Hendrix, 1980; Kutchai, 1998; Tso, 1995). Hydrochloric acid, however, is a
strong acid with a high dissociation constant. It quickly and completely dissociates
in an aqueous solution into hydrogen and chloride ions. Although it is correct to
imagine that gastric juice is a fluid rich in these ions, it is incorrect to suggest that
it contains HCl (Forte & Wolosin, 1987; McGuigan, 1987; Sachs, 1987). This is
not a trivial distinction. As emphasized throughout this book, precise information
about the ionic composition of aqueous solutions and body fluids is essential to
understand relationships between independent and dependent variables, as well as
to determine how a solution's acidity is established. There are great, fundamental
differences between the concept that there is an undissociated molecule (HCl) in
the stomach lumen, and the concept that its contents contain high concentrations
of hydrogen and chloride ions.

Figure 5-16 is a gamblegram for gastric juice.

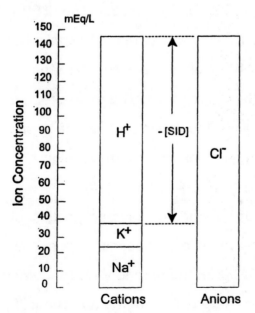

Figure 5-16 Gastric juice ionic
composition. [SID] is negative
because $[Cl^-] > ([Na^+] + [K^+])$.

Data in Figure 5-16 show that although total concentrations of anions and cations are equal, as it is in all biological fluids, the strong anion concentration ($[Cl^-]$) exceeds that of the sum of the strong cations ($[Na^+] + [K^+]$). This results in a negative value for the strong ion difference ($-[SID]$). When $[SID]$ is negative in an aqueous solution, hydrogen ions become the predominant weak cation and $[H^+] = -[SID]$ (Chapter 2, Section C.3.; Figure 2-5).

For gastric juice (Figure 5-16), chloride ions predominate as the anion, whereas in interstitial fluid (Figure 5-13), $[SID]$ is positive and $[HCO_3^-]$ is equal to $[SID]$. Interstitial fluid and gastric juice are similar in that neither fluid contains weak, non-volatile acids, but both are exposed to $CO_2$. Equation 29 shows the dependence of hydrogen ion concentration on the independent variables $[SID]$ and $PCO_2$.

Several complex explanations speculate as to how gastric juice is formed to be so acidic (Forte & Wolosin, 1987; Buchan, 1989; Tso, 1995; Guyton & Hall, 1996; Kutchai, 1998).. Although HION concepts readily explain how gastric juice is formed to be strongly acidic (Section B.1.2.), several other, different and more complex explanations have been proposed. The main problem to solve physiologically is how do cells in the wall of the stomach secrete a fluid whose concentrations of hydrogen and chloride ions are so high.

Traditional explanations of how gastric juice contains such high concentrations of hydrogen and chloride ions focus on proposed ionic exchange mechanisms at the interface of the parietal cell's apical membrane with the lumen of the secretory canaliculi and at the cell's basolateral membrane and the ECF. Common to all hypotheses, blood flow to the organ provides a source for ions being transferred by the parietal cell to the lumen of the canaliculi and serves also as a sink for movement in the opposite direction, from canaliculi lumen to blood. Figure 5-17 summarizes major traditional concepts.

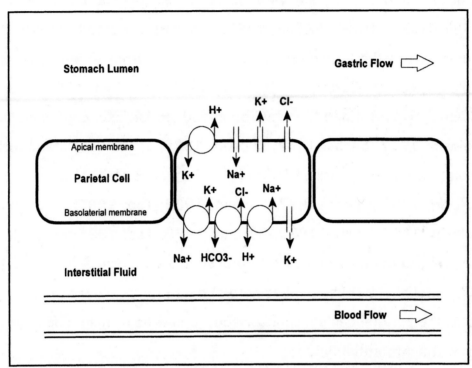

**Figure 5-17:** Traditional Concepts for Gastric Juice Secretion

It is commonly proposed, for example, without direct evidence that ATP-driven ion exchange, which is purported to occur at the apical membrane, pumps hydrogen ions into the gut lumen and potassium ions into the parietal cell (Forte & Wolosin, 1987; Sachs, 1987; McGuigan, 1987; Buchan, 1989; Tso, 1995; Guyton & Hall, 1996; Kutchai, 1998). It is suggested that hydrogen ion concentration in the parietal cell itself, however, comes from the dissociation of water (Equation 3; Buchan, 1989; Tso, 1995; Guyton & Hall, 1996) or from the carbon dioxide hydration reaction (Equation 22; McGuigan, 1987; Sachs, 1987; Kutchai, 1998). Intraluminal chloride ion concentration arises either from passive, or active mechanisms at the apical membrane (Forte & Wolosin, 1987; Sachs, 1987;

Buchan, 1989; Tso, 1995; Guyton & Hall, 1996; Kutchai, 1998).

Also, chloride ions are proposed to enter the parietal cell from extracellular fluid at the basolateral membrane by a chloride-bicarbonate coupled exchanger (Forte & Wolosin, 1987; Sachs, 1987; Buchan, 1989; Tso, 1995; Kutchai, 1998). Further, ion movements across the basolateral membrane come from sodium-potassium (Forte & Wolosin, 1987; Sachs, 1987; Buchan, 1989; Tso, 1995; Guyton & Hall, 1996; Kutchai, 1998) and from hydrogen-sodium ion exchange mechanisms (Forte & Wolosin, 1987; Sachs, 1987; Buchan, 1989) at the basolateral membrane. Also, channels have been described for sodium (Guyton & Hall, 1996), potassium (Forte & Wolosin, 1987; Sachs, 1987; Buchan, 1989; Tso, 1995), and chloride (Forte & Wolosin, 1987; Sachs, 1987; Buchan, 1989; Tso, 1995; Kutchai, 1998) ions at the apical cell membrane, and for potassium ions (Forte & Wolosin, 1987; Sachs, 1987; Kutchai, 1998) at the basolateral membrane. Flow of gastric juice renews fluid at the parietal cell's apical surface. Blood flow maintains ionic composition of the interstitial fluid.

### B.1.2. HION Concepts for Gastric Juice Formation

HION concepts simply explain the high hydrogen ion concentration of gastric juice based solely on its strong ion composition (Figures 5-16 and 5-18; Davenport, 1977; Hendrix, 1980; Buchan, 1989; Tso, 1995; Kutchai, 1998). It requires recognizing that $[H^+]$ is a dependent variable in body fluids devoid of non-volatile weak acids. It is driven by the independent

> Compare the simplicity and directness of HION explanations for the mechanisms underlying gastric juice's low pH, to the unnecessarily more complex ones promoted in many textbooks.

variables $PCO_2$ and [SID] (Equation 29). Also, $PCO_2$ has little effect, because, as for all other body fluids, dissolved carbon dioxide diffuses rapidly along a partial pressure gradient through all aqueous solutions and across all cell membranes. There is a simple explanation for the high hydrogen ion concentration of gastric juice. It depends entirely on a negative [SID], the concentration difference between its strong cations and its strong anions (Figure 5-16).

Sodium and potassium ions are the strong cations in gastric juice; chloride ions are its only strong anion (Figure 5-16). Their difference in concentration defines [SID] (Chapter 2, Sections C.2. and C.3.). This ionic composition profile is qualitatively the same for gastric juice, even though its absolute

> HION concepts readily explain solely on the basis of its [SID] how gastric juice is so highly acidic.

concentrations of strong ions vary as a function of its formation rate (Figure 5-18; Davenport, 1977; Hendrix, 1980; Buchan, 1989; Tso, 1995; Kutchai, 1998).

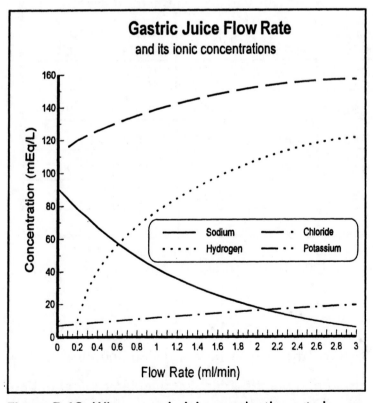

**Figure 5-18:** When gastric juice production rate is near zero, [SID] is about -39 mEq/L. When it is near 3.0 ml/min, [SID] is about -129 mEq/L.

The gamblegram for gastric juice (Figure 5-16) is constructed for when its flow rate is nominally 1.0 ml/min.  Other, similar diagrams could be constructed for different flow rates, because the relative ionic composition of gastric juice depends on how fast it is secreted (Figure 5-18).  Even so, all would report a negative [SID]. As predicted by the relationships in Figure 5-18, [SID] would be less negative with lower formation rates, and *vice versa*.  Also, hydrogen ion concentration would increase with higher flow rates, and *vice versa*.

How high is the concentration of hydrogen ions in gastric juice depends on its flow rate, but it is always quantitatively dependent on the solution's negative [SID] (See Table 5-3).  This is a central issue in understanding HION concepts.

| [SID]<br>(mEq/L) | [H$^+$]<br>(mEq/L) | pH | [OH$^-$]<br>(pEq/L) | [HCO$_3^-$]<br>(nEq/L) |
|---|---|---|---|---|
| -84 | 84 | 1.076 | 0.5 | 14.6 |
| -86 | 86 | 1.066 | 0.5 | 14.3 |
| -88 | 88 | 1.056 | 0.5 | 14.0 |
| -90 | 90 | 1.046 | 0.5 | 13.7 |
| -92 | 92 | 1.036 | 0.5 | 13.4 |
| -94 | 94 | 1.027 | 0.5 | 13.1 |

**Table 5-3: Effect of an Increasing Negative [SID] on Dependent Variables in Gastric Juice***

\* $PCO_2 = 50$ Torr; $K'_w = 4.4 \cdot 10^{-14} (Eq/L)^2$; $K_3 = 6.0 \cdot 10^{-11} Eq/L$; $K_c = 2.46 \cdot 10^{-11} (Eq/L)^2/Torr$ (modified from Stewart, 1981)

Data in Table 5-3 show  the effects of increasing negative [SID]'s on the hydrogen ion concentration in gastric juice, as calculated by equation 29. The data indicate that when [SID] is negative, [H$^+$] = -[SID] and as [SID] negativity increases, [H$^+$] increases and pH decreases (Figure 5-16; Figure 2-5). The initial value of [SID] = -84 mEq/L was estimated from data in Figure 5-18 at a flow of 1 ml/min and the increasing negativity would correspond with increased flow rate. The other independent variable, PCO$_2$, was held constant at 50 Torr, a representative tissue value. When the dependent variable ([H$^+$]) is known, pH and the other dependent variables, hydroxyl and bicarbonate ion concentrations, can be calculated using equations 6 and 22, respectively. These data also show that their values are too small to be shown in Figure 5-16.

HION concepts predict that the hydrogen ion concentration of gastric juice increases for one of two reasons, with both possibly operating simultaneously. The negative SID of gastric juice increases when the sum of its strong cations (sodium and potassium; Figure 5-16) decreases and the concentration

> Gastric juice acidity increases when its sum of strong cations decreases and/or when its chloride ion concentration increases. Both effects operate by making [SID] more negative.

of chloride ions remains unchanged. It also increases when chloride ion concentration increases and the sum of strong cations remains constant. Negative SID would increase even more when these same cationic and anionic mechanisms operate at the same time. Processes which control these strong ion concentrations are already documented in traditional explanations for how gastric juice is formed (Figure 5-17).

Both active and passive transport mechanisms have been proposed to operate at the parietal cell's apical surface which would decrease gastric juice sodium and potassium ion concentrations, as well as increase its chloride ion concentration (Forte & Wolosin, 1987; Sachs, 1987; Buchan,1989; Tso, 1995; Guyton & Hall, 1996; Kutchai, 1998). The pivotal and defining event, however, in defining the acidity of gastric juice is the effect of strong ionic concentrations in establishing its negative SID.

Traditional concepts usually explain interactions across membranes as exchanges of strong cations, such as $Na^+$ and $K^+$, for $H^+$ and exchanges of the strong anion, $Cl^-$ for $HCO_3^-$ (Figure 5-17). A "$Na^+/H^+$ exchanger"(Forte & Wolosin, 1987, Sachs, 1987; Schulz, 1987; Tanner, 1995; Petersen, 1987), "$K^+/H^+$ antiport" (Buchan, 1989; Kutchai, 1998; Forte & Wolosin, 1987; Ganong, 1997; Tanner, 1995; Guyton & Hall, 1996), "$Cl^-/HCO_3^-$ exchanger" (Petersen, 1987; Tanner, 1995; Ganong, 1997; Forte & Wolosin, 1987; Sachs, 1987;Schulz, 1987;Tso, 1995), "active transport or secretion of $H^+$"(Schulz, 1987; Guyton & Hall, 1996;Tanner, 1995; Rose & Post, 2001; Davenport, 1977; Abelow, 1998), "$HCO_3^-$ reabsorption" (Guyton & Hall, 1996; Tanner, 1995; Rose & Post, 2001; Davenport, 1977; Abelow, 1998) are terms used to explain ion movements between fluid compartments separated by a membrane.

The implicit assumption seems to be that in order to preserve electrical neutrality in each solution, there is an obligation to exchange ions of the same charge across the membrane separating them. This is an invalid and unnecessary proposal. Also implied is that if $[H^+]$ increases in one of the fluids, the hydrogen ions had to come from the fluid on the other side of the membrane by some metabolically linked process in the membrane. This is also an unnecessary assumption. These descriptions are metaphors which fail to give a complete picture of the involved processes ( Fencl & Leith, 1993).

The analyses described in this book and in other publications (Stewart, 1978; Stewart, 1983; Fencl & Leith, 1993; Jones, 1987, 1990, 1997) use HION concepts to explain these phenomena. These concepts use principles of electrical neutrality and equilibrium constraints on dissociation reactions to describe ionic composition of body fluids. They also identify which factors are dependent and which are independent variables for establishing body fluid pH.

When two fluid compartments are separated by a membrane, several basic ideas and principles put constraints on each of the fluids. The parietal cell apical membrane, for example, separates ductal lumen fluid from intracellular fluid. Regardless of gastric fluid flow rate, chloride concentration is greater than the sum of sodium and potassium concentrations in ductal fluid (see Fig. 5-18; Buchan, 1989; Hendrix, 1980; Tso, 1995; Kutchai, 1998). This produces a negative [SID] in the gastric fluid. If both [Cl$^-$]and [K$^+$] remained constant and [Na$^+$] were reduced by the active transport of sodium ions from the ductal fluid into the parietal cell, the lumen [SID] would become more negative, and the cell's [SID] would become more positive. The strong ion difference is an independent variable which determines the concentration of dependent variables (i.e. [H$^+$], [OH$^-$], [HCO$_3^-$], [CO$_3^{2-}$]) in both the ductal fluid and the parietal cell fluid. Since [SID] has been changed in both the luminal fluid and in the parietal cell's fluid, the dependent variable concentrations will be determined by the following physical and chemical constraints:

1) electroneutrality must be maintained in each solution.
2) equilibrium constraints of the dissociation reactions in which the dependent variables participate.

These constraints increase as the complexity of the solution's components increases. Intracellular fluid (Fig. 5-15) contains non-volatile weak acids and has a large positive [SID] while gastric juice contains no non-volatile weak acids and has a negative [SID]. The solution for [H$^+$] which secondarily allows solution for all dependent variable concentrations and also assures electrical neutrality, is a third-order equation in gastric juice (Chapter 3, Equation 29) and a fourth-order equation in parietal cell fluid (Chapter 4, Equation 42).

### B.1.3. The Alkaline Tide

It is well documented that blood leaving the gut is more alkaline after eating, than it is prior to a meal (Abelow, 1998; Ganong, 1997; Tso, 1995). This phenomenon is indirectly linked to the reflex increase in gastric juice formation triggered by eating. Data in Figure 5-18 show that when

> The well documented alkaline tide seen in blood leaving the gut after a meal is directly related to the ionic mechanisms, which give gastric juice its characteristic

there is an increase in the formation rate of gastric juice, its concentration of sodium ions decreases and that of its chloride ions increases. The combined effect is to increase its negative [SID] and increase hydrogen ion concentration (Table 5-3). We propose that the consequent increase in the parietal cell's sodium ion concentration and its decrease in chloride ion concentration are met by ion fluxes first from interstitial fluid at its basolateral surface, then from perfusing blood, which serves as both a renewing source and a sink of electrolytes (Figure 5-17).

The increased flux of sodium ions into blood perfusing the gut after eating and the outflux of chloride ions from it increases plasma [SID] and consequently decreases its hydrogen ion concentration (Table 5-4; Figure 5-14).

Data in Table 5-4 show the effects of increasing [SID] on the hydrogen ion concentration in plasma as calculated by Equation 42. The other independent variable, $PCO_2$ was held constant at 40 Torr, a representative systemic arterial value. Although $PCO_2$ would increase in blood as it passed through metabolizing tissue, the effect would be to moderate the decrease in $[H^+]$ and the increase in $[HCO_3^-]$ shown here. Also, a change in $[A^-]$ (See Figure 5-14; Chapter 4, Section B) due to the change in pH would also influence the values shown in Table 5-4.

| Table 5-4: Effect of Increasing Plasma [SID] on Dependent Variable Concentrations* | | | | |
|---|---|---|---|---|
| [SID] (mEq/L) | [$H^+$] (nEq/L) | pH | [$OH^-$] ($\mu$Eq/L) | [$HCO_3^-$] (mEq/L) |
| 42 | 39 | 7.409 | 1.1 | 25.2 |
| 44 | 36 | 7.439 | 1.2 | 27.0 |
| 46 | 34 | 7.467 | 1.3 | 28.9 |
| 48 | 32 | 7.494 | 1.4 | 30.7 |
| 50 | 30 | 7.520 | 1.5 | 32.6 |
| 52 | 29 | 7.544 | 1.5 | 34.4 |

\* $PCO_2 = 40$ Torr; $[A_{TOT}] = 20.0$ mmol/L; $K'_w = 4.4 \cdot 10^{-14} (Eq/L)^2$

$K_c = 2.46 \cdot 10^{-11} (Eq/L)^2/Torr$; $K_3 = 6.0 \cdot 10^{-11} Eq/L$; $K_a = 2 \cdot 10^{-7} Eq/L$

(modified from Stewart, 1981)

The concentration of bicarbonate ion, hydrogen ion and the other dependent variables in plasma change as functions of plasma [SID], and to a lesser extent, to the small changes in $PCO_2$ that occur as blood perfuses metabolizing tissue. For the same reasons as outlined in the previous section, the dependent variables are internal to a given fluid compartment and their concentration values represent the fluid's reaction to the externally imposed values of the independent variables ( Fencl & Leith, 1993; Stewart, 1983; Jones, 1997). The [$HCO_3^-$] and [$OH^-$] increase and the [$H^+$] decreases in plasma only as an obligation to the increase in plasma [SID]. There is no reason to propose that bicarbonate concentration increases because of an ion exchange phenomenon, or that [$HCO_3^-$] itself is responsible for the alkalinity of gastric venous blood. Bicarbonate concentration is a passive consequence, not a causative effect.

> The bicarbonate ion concentration in gastric venous blood is the result, not the cause, of the ionic mechanisms associated with gastric juice formation.

The postprandial alkaline tide is simply explained solely on HION concepts. The pivotal issue underlying both the acidity of gastric juice and the alkalinity of blood leaving the stomach after a meal is the physical chemical relationship between [SID] and hydrogen ion concentration for an aqueous solution. More complex explanations (Figure 5-17) are unnecessary.

## B.2. Pancreatic Juice

The previous section used HION concepts to explain the normal, high acidity of gastric juice. This section uses the same principles to describe the mechanisms by which pancreatic juice is so strongly alkaline, with a pH of 7.6 to 8.3 (Guyton & Hall, 1996; Davenport, 1977). It also explains how bicarbonate ion concentration in pancreatic juice can be as high as five to six times that of arterial plasma (Guyton & Hall, 1996;Kutchai, 1998; Tso, 1995; Davenport, 1977). Pancreatic juice also contains the enzymes, trypsin, chymotrypsin and carboxypolypeptidase, for digesting dietary protein, pancreatic lipase, cholesterol esterase and phospholipase, for digesting fats and pancreatic amylase for digesting carbohydrates.

Data in Figure 5-19 show that the sum of the strong cations ($[Na^+] + [K^+]$) exceeds that of the strong anion concentration ($[Cl^-]$), resulting in a positive value for the strong ion difference ([SID]). When [SID] is positive in an aqueous solution containing $CO_2$, bicarbonate ions become the predominant weak anion and $[HCO_3^-] = [SID]$ (Figure 3-8; Figure 5-13). Interstitial fluid and

> Sodium ions are the predominant strong cation and chloride ions are the predominant strong anion in pancreatic juice.

gastric juice are similar to pancreatic juice in that they are all exposed to $CO_2$ but are lacking weak non-volatile acids. Equation 29 shows the dependence of hydrogen ion concentration on the independent variables, [SID] and $PCO_2$.

The gamblegram for pancreatic juice is shown in Figure 5-19.

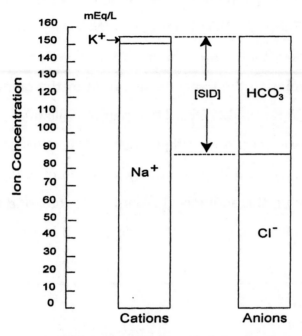

**Figure 5-19** Pancreatic juice ionic composition

### B.2.1. Traditional Concepts of Pancreatic Juice Formation

All proposals which attempt to explain the composition of pancreatic juice must account for its high pH and for its high concentration of bicarbonate ions. Many traditional concepts argue that its high pH comes directly and causally from the high concentration of bicarbonate ions. HION concepts describe, in contrast, that both characteristics are obligations of the strong ion difference in pancreatic juice, and that they are independently established dependent variables. A similar explanation was presented for how the high concentration of hydrogen ions arose from the negative [SID] of gastric juice (Figure 5-16).

The mechanisms involved in pancreatic exocrine secretions are less certain than those reported for gastric juice partially because of differing experimental findings from studies using different experimental preparations and experimental stimuli in different animal species (Schulz, 1987; Hootman & Williams, 1987; Petersen, 1987).  It is generally agreed that one of the main functions of pancreatic acinar cells is to contribute enzymes to the exocrine secretion of the gland (Buchan, 1989; Hendrix, 1980; Tso, 1995; Kutchai, 1998; Hootman & Williams, 1987; Schulz, 1987).  The acinar cells also contribute a fluid "rich in NaCl" (Hootman & Williams, 1987; Schulz, 1987; Kutchai, 1998), presumably sodium and chloride ions. Modification of this fluid with the addition of bicarbonate ions and loss of chloride ions is attributed to the pancreatic duct cells, as illustrated in Figure 5-20.

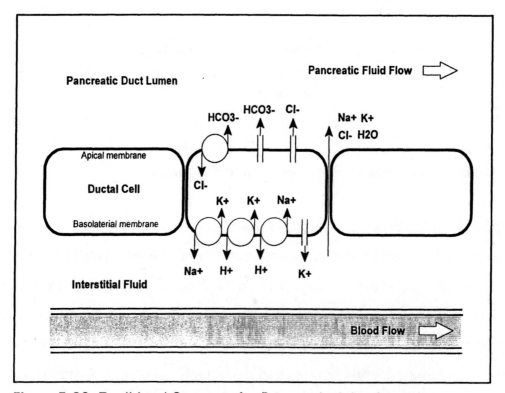

**Figure 5-20:** Traditional Concepts for Pancreatic Juice Secretion

Traditional explanations of how pancreatic juice contains such a high concentration of bicarbonate ions and low concentration of chloride ions focus on exchange mechanisms at both the duct cell's apical and basolateral membranes. It is proposed by some that an ion exchange mechanism at the apical membrane moves bicarbonate into the duct lumen and chloride ions into the ductal cell (Buchan, 1989; Tso, 1995; Kutchai, 1998;Schulz, 1987). To supplement this mechanism, ion channels move both bicarbonate (Buchan, 1989;Schulz, 1987) and chloride (Kutchai, 1998) from cell to lumen. It is proposed (Buchan, 1989;Guyton & Hall, 1996;Tso, 1995;Kutchai, 1998;Schulz, 1987) that bicarbonate is formed in the ductal cell from the $CO_2$ hydration reaction (See Figure 3-6).

The $CO_2$ hydration reaction also produces a hydrogen ion which is removed from the cell at the basolateral surface by either a sodium-hydrogen antiport (Buchan, 1989; Guyton & Hall, 1996; Kutchai, 1998; Schulz, 1987) or a $K^+$, $H^+$ ATPase (Kutchai, 1998). Since the sodium-hydrogen antiport exchanges cellular $H^+$ for $Na^+$, a sodium-potassium ATPase on the basolateral membrane removes $Na^+$ from the cell (Buchan, 1989; Tso, 1995; Schulz, 1987). If the $K^+$, $H^+$ ATPase on the basolateral membrane is more appealing, a $K^+$-channel provides extracellular $K^+$ to keep it running (Kutchai, 1998). Some propose that $Na^+$, $K^+$, $Cl^-$ and water reach lumenal fluid by a paracellular route (Tso, 1995) but others hypothesize this route only for the two cations (Schulz, 1987; Buchan, 1989; Kutchai, 1998).

### B.2.2. HION Concepts of Pancreatic Juice Formation

HION concepts explain simply why bicarbonate ion concentration is high and hydrogen ion concentration is low in pancreatic juice. For pancreatic juice, as for gastric juice, non-volatile weak acids ($[A_{TOT}]$) are not present. This leaves [SID] and $PCO_2$ as the only independent variables which affect the concentrations of dependent variables such as hydrogen and bicarbonate ions. Also, carbon dioxide diffuses rapidly along a partial pressure gradient through all aqueous solutions and across all cell membranes.  The high bicarbonate ion concentration in pancreatic juice depends virtually entirely on the difference between its strong cations and its strong anions, defined as its positive [SID] (Figure 5-19; Chapter 2, Section C.2.).

> Pancreatic juice's bicarbonate ion concentration and its characteristic high pH are direct results of its [SID].

The total concentration of all cations and anions must equal one another in pancreatic juice to maintain its electrical neutrality, as it must for any other aqueous solution (Figure 5-19).  This means that with a constant concentration of strong cations ($Na^+$ and $K^+$), as the concentration of the strong

> Pancreatic juice's characteristics of constant concentration of strong cations and its reciprocal relationship between bicarbonate and chloride ions are independent of its production rate.

anion ($Cl^-$) in pancreatic juice falls, its bicarbonate ion concentration will increase (Figure 5-19).  The constant concentration of the strong cations and the reciprocal relationship between bicarbonate and chloride ion concentrations for pancreatic juice is retained, regardless of the rate at which it is secreted (Figure 5-21; Buchan, 1989; Hendrix, 1980; Tso, 1995; Kutchai, 1998; Schulz, 1987).

Bicarbonate ion concentration in pancreatic juice is, in fact, equal to its [SID] (Figure 5-19; Table 5-5) as it was for interstitial fluid (Figure 5-13; Figure 3-8). This is a parallel relationship to that for hydrogen  ion concentration and negative [SID] in gastric  juice (Figure 5-16; Table 5-3 ), for similar physical chemical constraints, namely that: 1) electroneutrality of each solution be maintained; and 2) dissociation equilibria for all weakly dissociated dependent variables (i.e. $H^+$, $OH^-$, $HCO_3^-$ and $CO_3^{2-}$) in each solution be satisfied.

The effect of pancreatic juice flow rate on its ionic composition is shown in Figure 21.

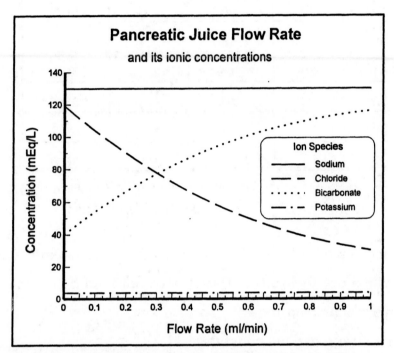

**Figure 5-21:** When pancreatic fluid flow rate is near zero, [SID] is about 15 mEq/L. When it is near 1.0 ml/min., [SID] is about 103 mEq/L.

The pivotal mechanism for increasing pancreatic juice's bicarbonate ion concentration is to increase [SID] by reducing its chloride ion concentration.

Data in Table 5-5 show the effects of increasing positive [SID] on the bicarbonate and other dependent variable concentrations in pancreatic juice, as calculated by Equation 29. The initial [SID] = 57 mEq/L was estimated from Figure 5-21 at a flow rate of 0.3 ml/min. The other independent variable, $PCO_2$, was held constant at 50 Torr, a representative value for a metabolizing tissue. The data show that when [SID] is positive, $[HCO_3^-]$ = [SID]. In addition, as [SID] becomes more positive, $[H^+]$ decreases and the solution becomes more alkaline.

| Table 5-5: Effect of Increasing [SID] on Dependent Variables in Pancreatic Juice* | | | | |
|---|---|---|---|---|
| [SID] (mEq/L) | [H$^+$] (nEq/L) | pH | [OH$^-$] ($\mu$Eq/L) | [HCO$_3^-$] (mEq/L) |
| 57 | 22 | 7.665 | 2.0 | 56.8 |
| 59 | 21 | 7.680 | 2.1 | 58.8 |
| 61 | 20 | 78.694 | 2.2 | 60.8 |
| 63 | 20 | 7.708 | 2.2 | 62.8 |
| 65 | 19 | 7.722 | 2.3 | 64.8 |
| 67 | 18 | 7.735 | 2.4 | 66.8 |

\* $PCO_2 = 50$ Torr; $K'_w = 4.4 \bullet 10^{-14} (Eq/L)^2$; $K_3 = 6.0 \bullet 10^{-11} Eq/L$

$K_c = 2.46 \bullet 10^{-11} (Eq/L)^2/Torr$ (modifed from Stewart, 1981)

The pivotal mechanism for increasing the alkalinity of pancreatic juice, is to make a solution with a positive [SID]. This is accomplished by reducing its chloride concentration while maintaining the concentration of its strong cations constant (See Figure 5-21; Buchan, 1989; Hendrix, 1980; Tso, 1995; Kutchai, 1998; Schulz, 1987). The consequent changes in the

The high pH and the alkalinity of pancreatic juice are direct consequences of its positive [SID].

concentrations of dependent variables (i.e. H$^+$, OH$^-$, HCO$_3^-$ and CO$_3^{2-}$) are secondary to the changes in [SID] and/or PCO$_2$ as determined by Equation 29. It is unnecessary, in fact wrong, to explain interactions across membranes as exchanges of a strong anion (i.e. Cl$^-$) for a weak anion (i.e. HCO$_3^-$) or to imagine a membrane channel which is specific for a weak anion as is traditionally done (See Figure 5-20). Moving a strong anion, alone, which results in a change in an independent variable, [SID], will produce a change in the concentration of all the dependent variables in the solution (See Section B.1.2.).

### B.2.3. The Acid Tide

Analogous to the increased alkalinity of blood leaving the stomach, which produces an "alkaline tide" (See Section B.1.3.), there is an acid tide in blood draining the pancreas ( Abelow, 1998; Tso, 1995). Many propose that the bicarbonate ion in the ductal lumen originates from the $CO_2$ hydration

> Analogous to the ionic mechanisms, which produce the postprandial alkaline tide in gastric venous blood, an acid tide in pancreatic venous blood mirrors the ionic mechanisms, which give pancreatic juice its characteristic high pH.

reaction in the ductal cell (Buchan, 1989; Guyton & Hall, 1996; Tso, 1995; Kutchai, 1998;Schulz, 1987); a mechanism is needed to remove the hydrogen ion, also produced by this reaction. In Figure 5-20 both a $Na^+/H^+$ (Buchan, 1989; Guyton & Hall, 1996; Tso, 1995; Kutchai, 1998; Schulz, 1987) and a $K^+/H^+$ antiport (Kutchai, 1998) are proposed for moving hydrogen ions from the ductal cell to the extracellular fluid.

HION concepts propose that anything which would decrease [SID] in blood would cause its $[H^+]$ to increase. If $[Cl^-]$ in blood remained constant, then removing sodium and/or potassium from extracellular fluid into the ductal cell by an active transport or cation channel would decrease [SID] in plasma. If sodium and potassium concentrations in blood remained constant and the chloride ions being removed from lumenal fluid were transferred to plasma, this would also reduce plasma [SID] and increase $[H^+]$ in blood leaving the pancreas. Traditional concepts show no mechanism which moves chloride ions from lumenal fluid to extracellular fluid, although this might be the most plausible since $[Cl^-]$ in lumenal fluid is being reduced (Figure 5-21) and blood flowing through the organ provides an infinite sink for this ion. The effect of decreasing [SID] in plasma is shown in Table 5-6.

| Table 5-6: Effect of Decreasing Plasma [SID] on Dependent Variable Concentrations* | | | | |
|---|---|---|---|---|
| [SID] (mEq/L) | [$H^+$] (nEq/L) | pH | [$OH^-$] [$\mu$Eq/L] | [$HCO_3^-$] (mEq/L) |
| 42 | 39 | 7.409 | 1.1 | 25.2 |
| 40 | 42 | 7.377 | 1.0 | 23.4 |
| 38 | 45 | 7.343 | 1.0 | 21.7 |
| 36 | 49 | 7.307 | 0.9 | 19.9 |
| 34 | 54 | 7.268 | 0.8 | 18.2 |
| 32 | 59 | 7.226 | 0.7 | 16.6 |

\* $PCO_2 = 40$ Torr; [$A_{TOT}$] = 20.0 mmol/L; $K'_w = 4.4 \cdot 10^{-14}$ (Eq/L)$^2$;

$K_c = 2.46 \cdot 10^{-11}$ (Eq/L)$^2$/Torr; $K_3 = 6.0 \cdot 10^{-11}$ Eq/L;

$K_a = 2.0 \cdot 10^{-7}$ Eq/L (modified from Stewart, 1981)

Data in Table 5-6 show the effect of decreasing [SID] on the concentrations of hydrogen ion and other dependent variables in plasma as calculated using Equation 42. Initial [SID] was 42 mEq/L (Stewart, 1981) and $PCO_2$ was held constant at a normal systemic arterial value, 40 Torr. The data show that as [SID] decreases in plasma, [$H^+$] increases, while pH and [$HCO_3^-$] decrease. These data support a simple mechanism for increasing [$HCO_3^-$] in pancreatic duct fluid while increasing [$H^+$] in blood leaving the pancreas.

Data in Figures 5-19 and 5-21 show that when strong cations in ductal fluid are constant, there is an increase in ductal fluid [SID] because of a decrease in its [$Cl^-$] as the mechanism for the [$HCO_3^-$] increases. A mechanism which transfers the chloride removed from ductal fluid to blood perfusing the pancreas would have the effect of decreasing plasma [SID], thereby raising the [$H^+$] in blood leaving the organ. Changing the concentration of one strong anion in both fluids accounts for the changes in the dependent variables, hydrogen and bicarbonate ions.

# Section C

## Main Points from Chapter 5

✔ The strong ion difference ([SID]) and $PCO_2$ are the independent variables which determine concentrations of the dependent variables, $[H^+]$ $[OH^-]$, $[HCO_3^-]$ and $[CO_3^{2-}]$ in interstitial fluid, gastric juice and pancreatic juice.

✔ Carbon dioxide is very soluble and freely permeable in membranes leaving [SID] as the major determinant of dependent variable concentrations in body fluids free of non-volatile weak acids such as proteins and phosphates.

✔ In an aqueous solution containing strong ions and $CO_2$, if the concentration of strong anions is greater than that of the strong cations, [SID] is negative, the solution is acidic and $[H^+] = -[SID]$ and $[H^+] > [OH^-]$, $[HCO_3^-]$ and $[CO_3^{2-}]$. This is what happens in the formation of gastric juice.

✔ In an aqueous solution containing strong ions and $CO_2$, if the concentration of strong cations is greater than that of the strong anions, [SID] is positive, the solution is basic and the concentration of weak anions is greater than $[H^+]$. This is what happens in the formation of pancreatic juice.

✔ Moving a strong anion, such as chloride, from one solution (A) across a membrane into a second solution (B) will cause [SID] to change in both solutions. [SID] in solution (A) will become more positive, and its $[H^+]$ will decrease, while [SID] in solution (B) will become less positive and its $[H^+]$ will increase.

# Chapter 6

## Acid-Base Pathophysiology

**What to Look for:**

In this chapter you will learn about:

- traditional concepts for determining "whole body" acid-base status based on analyses of blood plasma
- traditional diagnostic criteria for determining respiratory acidosis and alkalosis
- traditional diagnostic criteria for determining non-respiratory acidosis and alkalosis
- the diagnostic role of the anion gap in traditional acid-base disturbances
- HION criteria for determining respiratory acidosis and alkalosis
- HION criteria for determining non-respiratory acidosis and alkalosis
- how HION concepts clarify diagnosis of acid-base disturbances

This chapter applies HION concepts to respiratory and non-respiratory ("metabolic") acid-base derangements. Analyses of plasma are commonly used clinically to reflect acid-base status and the whole body distribution of water, as well as to reveal respiratory and non-respiratory ("metabolic") compensations to physiological stressors. More commonly used analyses, like the gaseous and electrolyte composition of plasma, for example, are considered to index " whole body" acid-base status.

Traditional interpretations rely heavily on the components of the Henderson-Hasselbalch equation (i.e. $[HCO_3^-]$, pH and $PCO_2$; Equation 24 and 61) or its many graphical and interpretative forms. As for Chapter 5, emphasis in this chapter will be placed on using analyses of the two independent variables, $PCO_2$ and [SID]. In addition, the separation of $[A_{TOT}]$ into its two major components,

> HION concepts are a more complete basis for describing the ionic mechanisms for determining acid-base status, than are most traditional hypotheses.

inorganic phosphate ($[P_i]$) and plasma albumin concentration ([Alb]) (Chapter 4, Sections C.2. and D) will be used in the analysis.

# Section A

## Diagnostic Techniques

Acid-base disturbances are commonly diagnosed by analyses of anaerobically drawn, systemic arterial blood samples. Most clinical laboratories use thermostated electrodes to detect pH and $PCO_2$, then depend on Equations 24 and 61, the Henderson-Hasselbalch equation, to calculate $[HCO_3^-]$. Some report a value for "Total $CO_2$" or just "$CO_2$", rather than one for $[HCO_3^-]$

> Commonly used clinical analyses for bicarbonate ion concentration in blood plasma, measure [Total $CO_2$]. The implied assumption that $[HCO_3^-]$ = [Total $CO_2$] is incorrect.

because there is no chemical method for measuring $[HCO_3^-]$ in an aqueous sample (Cohen & Kassirer, 1982; Chinard, 1966). Carbon dioxide in all its chemical forms is determined by adding a strong acid to the plasma sample, which then releases

$CO_2$ as a gas (Fig. 3-6). Either a manometric or colorimetric technique measures the total $CO_2$ released from the plasma.

The common presumption that the released $CO_2$ represents $[HCO_3^-]$, however, is incorrect. Although about 95% of plasma $CO_2$ is assimilated in $[HCO_3^-]$, 5% is dissolved in plasma and contained in carbonate, carbonic acid and carbamino $CO_2$ (Abelow, 1998; Rose & Post, 2001; Cohen & Kassirer, 1982). Unfortunately, carbonic acid cannot be distinguished from dissolved $CO_2$ and carbamino $CO_2$ cannot be readily separated from bicarbonate (Chinard, 1966). Few textbooks distinguish among [Total $CO_2$],"measured $[HCO_3^-]$", and $[HCO_3^-]$ calculated based on measurements of $PCO_2$ and pH.

When the measurement of $[HCO_3^-]$ is based on a method that uses strong acid addition to a plasma or serum sample, as is used in modern sequential multichannel analyzers (SMA's), what is measured is [Total $CO_2$] and it unavoidably involves an inherent error which is seldom acknowledged (Abelow, 1998; Rose & Post, 2001). This means that whenever the term "$[HCO_3^-]$" appears in an expression, such as in the Henderson- Hasselbalch equation, it is likely to represent [total $CO_2$], but not $[HCO_3^-]$ itself.

Calculating $[HCO_3^-]$ using measured $PCO_2$ and pH or $[H^+]$, is valid for the first dissociation constant (or pK) of carbonic acid. Using the Henderson- Hasselbalch equation, though, to indicate cause-and-effect is wrong. Dependent variables in an equation

> Dependent variables (i.e. $H^+$, $HCO_3^-$ and $CO_3^{2-}$) in an equation may be correlated but they cannot determine each other.

(i.e. $[H^+]$, pH and $[HCO_3^-]$) may be correlated but they cannot determine each other. Hydrogen ion concentration is not determined by the value for bicarbonate, and *vice versa*. Also, the widespread presumption that $[HCO_3^-]$ or the ratio of

[HCO$_3^-$] to H$_2$CO$_3$ or to ($\alpha \bullet$PCO$_2$) determines [H$^+$] is incorrect . Calculation is not cause-and-effect; it is arithmetic (Stewart, 1978).

# Section B

## Challenges to Acid-Base Status

Systemic arterial blood at 37°C normally has a pH of about 7.40, with a range from 7.35-7.45, equivalent to a [H$^+$] of 45 to 36 nEq/L. Blood with a lower than normal pH is acidemic, and that with a higher than normal pH is alkalemic. Although plasma water at 37°C is acidic only when its pH is below 6.8 (the point of acid-base neutrality; Chapter 2, Section B), acidemia for biological fluids is usually defined differently. The primary cause of clinical conditions which result in pH's outside a normal range is typically evaluated by measuring plasma PaCO$_2$ and [HCO$_3^-$] (Total CO$_2$). Systemic arterial PCO$_2$ is normally 40 Torr with a range of 35 to 45 Torr. Normal plasma [HCO$_3^-$] is about 24 mEq/L with a range of 22 - 26 mEq/L. These are the ranges of normalcy usually quoted in textbooks and in clinical laboratory reports. Different ranges, though, are often referenced in the acid-base literature (Davenport, 1974;Stewart, 1981;Burtis and Ashwood, 1999; Braunwald et. al., 1987).

# Section C

## Respiratory Disorders

### C.1. Respiratory Acidosis

Systemic arterial pH and PCO$_2$ often change because of factors

> Changes in respiration have a powerful influence on whole body acid-base status, because of their effects on the concentration of carbon dioxide in plasma and eventually in all body fluids.

affecting respiration (Chapter 3, Section A). The influence is either by restricting alveolar ventilation, reducing lung perfusion, or weakening gas diffusion gradients. These effects occur in any combination. Airway obstruction, weakness of respiratory muscles by disease or by drug action, for example, lower alveolar ventilation in relation to $CO_2$ production (Equation 20). Also, pneumothorax, pulmonary edema , or emphysema compromise alveolar gas exchange in one way, or another (Abelow, 1998; Rose & Post, 2001).

Respiratory acidosis develops when alveolar ventilation is low relative to the body's carbon dioxide production (Equation 20; Jones, 1987). It is characterized by an increase in systemic arterial $PCO_2$ and $[H^+]$. Alveolar ventilation also decreases and plasma carbon dioxide increases as a compensation for non-respiratory ("metabolic") alkalosis, but $[H^+]$ is lower than normal. Changes in alveolar ventilation occur

> Hypoventilation reduces alveolar ventilation, induces hypercapnia and lowers body fluid pH to produce an acidosis.

rapidly (in seconds) and result in equally rapid changes in alveolar and systemic plasma $PaCO_2$. Effects on arterial plasma $[H^+]$ are also rapid. Any change in plasma $PCO_2$ alters partial pressure gradients and consequently diffusion flow rates, thereby changing interstitial $PCO_2$. This changes the gradient for $CO_2$, which affects $CO_2$ diffusion rate from inside metabolizing cells, the ultimate source of body $CO_2$ production, to circulating blood. Data in Figures 3-7,4-9, and 4-11 show that when $PCO_2$ changes in interstitial fluid, in plasma and intracellular fluid, $[H^+]$ changes also. In respiratory acidosis, the decreased alveolar ventilation leads to an increased $PCO_2$ and increased $[H^+]$ in all body fluids.

## C.2. Respiratory Alkalosis

Primary respiratory alkalosis (Chapter 3, Section A) is characterized by

hypocapnia, with $PaCO_2$ being less than 35
Torr, and there is an elevated pH because of
a lower-than-normal $[H^+]$. It is caused by
hyperventilation which may be emotionally
induced, or caused by hypoxemia or by
mechanical over-ventilation, as by an

> Hyperventilation increases alveolar ventilation, induces hypocapnia and raises body fluid pH to produce an alkalosis.

incorrectly set ventilator (Rose & Post, 2001; Abelow, 1998). Acute respiratory

alkalosis develops when there is an increase in alveolar ventilation (hyperventilation)

which is not a compensation for a condition of non-respiratory ("metabolic")

acidosis. It lowers $PaCO_2$ and $[H^+]$, but minimally decreases $[HCO_3^-]$.


Prolonged hyperventilation is characterized by paresthesias, typically including

tingling of the fingers and toes, muscle spasms, and by tetany. These signs and

symptoms are related to a decrease in $[Ca^{2+}]$ when $[CO_3^{2-}]$ rises above about $10^{-5}$

Eq/L. Carbonate concentration increases when $PaCO_2$ decreases (Jones, 1997;

Stewart, 1981).


## C.3. Traditional Concepts vs. HION Concepts


Traditional concepts for diagnosing acute respiratory acidosis and alkalosis are

similar to HION concepts in that they both evaluate systemic arterial pH and $PCO_2$.

Acute respiratory acidosis or acidemia is based on determinations of a higher- than-

normal systemic arterial $PCO_2$ and $[H^+]$ (low pH). Acute respiratory alkalosis or

alkalemia is based on determinations of a lower- than- normal systemic arterial

$PCO_2$ and $[H^+]$ (higher- than- normal pH). Traditional and HION concepts differ in

the importance each attributes to bicarbonate ion as a "buffer", or a means of

compensating for changes in hydrogen ion concentration caused by changes in

$PCO_2$.

Traditional concepts propose that with a chronic respiratory acidosis, kidney compensation adds more $H^+$'s to the urine and $HCO_3^-$'s to the blood. The kidneys compensate for respiratory alkalosis by excreting $HCO_3^-$ in the urine and by the reduced $PCO_2$

> Renal and respiratory reflexes reciprocally attempt to compensate for changes in plasma acid-base status.

accompanying the respiratory alkalosis reduces $H^+$ secretion by the kidney tubule epithelium (Davenport, 1974; Tanner, 1995; Guyton & Hall, 1996).

HION concepts consider both hydrogen ion and bicarbonate ions to be dependent variables (Stewart,1978,1983; Jones, 1990, 1997; Figge et. al. 1991, 1992; Fencl & Leith, 1993). Their concentrations are determined by two independent variables (e.g. $PCO_2$ and [SID]) in body fluids, which do not contain weak, non-volatile acids, such as interstitial fluid, gastric fluid and pancreatic fluid. Their concentrations are determined in blood plasma by four independent variables: $PCO_2$, [SID], albumin ([Alb]) and inorganic phosphate ($[P_i]$).

HION concepts propose that in chronic respiratory acidosis [SID] increases because of renal functions, which compensate for the elevated $[H^+]$. The renal compensation for respiratory acidosis is to increase plasma [SID] (i.e. making it more positive) by excreting chloride ion disproportionately more than sodium and potassium ions. By lowering plasma $[Cl^-]$, the concentration of bicarbonate increases with little change in non-volatile weak acid anions ($[A^-]$; Jones, 1997). The change in the concentration of the dependent variable, bicarbonate ion, is secondary to that of the independent variable, [SID] (Stewart, 1978, 1981; Fencl & Leith, 1993).

HION concepts propose that $[HCO_3^-]$ would change little in acute respiratory alkalosis, unless there is a decrease in systemic arterial [SID]. Sustained hyperventilation leads to renal excretion of chloride ion disproportionately less than sodium and potassium ions. This causes a rise in plasma [$Cl^-$] and a decrease in plasma [SID] (i.e. making it less positive), which will increase the concentration of the dependent variable, hydrogen ion ( Stewart, 1981; Jones, 1997). Also, lactate concentration, another strong anion, increases because of a stimulation of glycolysis in red blood cells and liver (Stewart, 1981).

Traditional concepts rely heavily on the Henderson-Hasselbalch equation in which two of the three variables are dependent variables (i.e. $H^+$ and $HCO_3^-$) whose concentrations are considered to be determined by only one series of reversible reactions (See Figure 3-6; also, Davenport, 1974) . HION concepts, on the other hand, consider that the concentrations of these two dependent variables are determined by several reactions which must be solved simultaneously to show how electrical neutrality is maintained in any body fluid system.

In respiratory acid-base disturbances, the independent variable, $PCO_2$ is the cause of the change in systemic arterial blood [$H^+$]. Since $CO_2$ is a very soluble and diffusible molecule, it readily penetrates membranes and changes [$H^+$] in all body fluid compartments. The non-volatile weak acids found in cells and those in plasma (i.e. [Alb], [$P_i$]) bind hydrogen ions, but their concentrations do not vary greatly . Non-reacting strongly dissociated ions, however, move across membranes separating two fluid compartments by known transport mechanisms. By influencing the strong ion difference in both fluid compartments, the concentrations of dependent variables in each compartment change (Chapter 5). This is a simpler and more logical explanation for renal compensation for disturbances of respiratory origin by manipulating [SID] in plasma and indirectly changing the concentrations of hydrogen ion and bicarbonate ion.

# Section D

# Non-respiratory ("Metabolic") Disorders

## D.1.Traditional Concepts

### D.1.1. Non-respiratory ("metabolic") alkalosis

Measurements of systemic arterial pH and [$HCO_3^-$] ([total $CO_2$]) are often used to identify primary non-respiratory (so-called "metabolic") pathologies. Non-respiratory alkalosis is indicated when arterial pH and plasma [$HCO_3^-$] are above normal. They come from the administration of $NaHCO_3$, loss of gastric juice by vomiting, low chloride intake, sweat losses in cystic fibrosis, prolonged heavy sweating with work or exercise or because of thiazide type diuretics,

> Loss of body water and electrolytes by vomiting, thiazide diuretics, excessive sweating without dietary replacements of lost water and electrolytes produce a state of non-respiratory, so-called "metabolic" alkalosis, which is characterized by higher-than-normal plasma [$HCO_3^-$]([total $CO_2$]) and pH.

or those which act on the loop of Henle (Abelow, 1998;Rose & Post, 2001 ). In general, any process or agent which produces a hypochloremia will cause non-respiratory ("metabolic") alkalosis (See Figure 5-14).

### D.1.2. Non-respiratory ("metabolic") acidosis

There is a so-called "metabolic" acidosis, when plasma [$HCO_3^-$] and arterial pH are both below normal (Davenport, 1974). The lower plasma [$HCO_3^-$] is often attributed to renal $HCO_3^-$ loss (Type 2 (proximal) renal tubular acidosis), "diminished H+ secretion (type 1 (distal) renal tubular acidosis)", loss of bicarbonate caused by diarrhea, or because of an "increased H+ load" due to lactic acidosis or ketoacidosis (Abelow, 1998; Rose & Post, 2001).  For example, a non-respiratory acidosis, which reduces plasma [$HCO_3^-$], is caused by an increase in [$Cl^-$] (hyperchloremic acidosis).

There are, however, other strong, and weak, acidic anions which cause non-respiratory acidosis, but they are not usually measured.  The strong anions lactate, sulfate, β-hydroxybutyrate, acetoacetate, as well as weak, non-volatile anions, like inorganic phosphate and serum albumin, contribute to non-respiratory disorders (See Figure 5-14; Chapter 4, Sections C & D).  The net effect of these unmeasured anions in plasma is often estimated by "the anion gap" (see Section E).

### D.2. Compensatory Mechanisms

### D.2.1. Non-respiratory ("Metabolic") Compensation for Respiratory Disorders

The partial pressure of carbon dioxide in  systemic arterial blood follows  quickly changes in ventilation.  Acute respiratory acidosis and alkalosis leave little time for compensation by non-respiratory ("metabolic") changes. The effects of  chronic respiratory acidosis or alkalosis are balanced by renal compensation.  The kidney is often described as responding to respiratory acidosis by retaining bicarbonate, resulting in increased plasma [$HCO_3^-$].  Its response to respiratory alkalosis is to increase the excretion of bicarbonate, which results in decreased plasma [$HCO_3^-$].  The common view of renal compensation for a respiratory acid-base disturbance is based on changes in plasma [$HCO_3^-$] controlled by the kidneys.

> Respiratory compensation for abnormal acid-base status operates much more quickly than does renal compensation.

### D.2.2. Respiratory Compensation for Non-respiratory ("Metabolic") Disorders

The effects of most non-respiratory acid-base disorders are quickly compensated by respiratory reflexes. The effect is to reduce, but not eliminate, the change in systemic arterial pH. Non-respiratory acidosis, for example, triggers within minutes an increase in

> Increased alveolar ventilation lowers arterial $PCO_2$, which compensates a non-respiratory acidosis. Hypoventilation compensates a non-respiratory alkalosis.

alveolar ventilation, with a consequent lowering of arterial $PCO_2$, which lessens the decrease in pH. The respiratory compensation to a non-respiratory alkalemia is a depressed ventilation causing $PaCO_2$ to increase and limit the rise in pH.

Neither respiratory, nor non-respiratory compensations are ever complete and never bring arterial blood pH back to a pH of 7.40. They do, however, reduce the condition of acidemia or alkalemia. Acid-base disturbances caused by a non-respiratory problem are partially compensated by a

> Neither renal, nor respiratory compensations for acid-base imbalance are complete, but only reduce the intensity of the acidemic or alkalemic state.

respiratory response. Disturbances caused by a respiratory problem are partially compensated by a non-respiratory, so-called "metabolic" response, but they are slower. It takes renal functions, for example, hours-to-days to provide partial compensations to acid-base perturbations coming from under-, or over-ventilation of the lungs.

## D.3. HION Concepts

### D.3.1. Non-respiratory Alkalosis

Non-respiratory disorders decrease plasma [H+] to produce an abnormally high pH. They arise from either an increase in plasma [SID], or a decrease in a plasma non-volatile weak acid, albumin ([Alb]).

### D.3.1.1. Non-respiratory Alkalosis Caused by Increase in Plasma [SID]

It may not be immediately apparent that just a change in a solution's water content also shifts its [H+] (pH). It does so by disproportionately affecting the difference between its concentrations of strong cations and strong anions, its strong ion difference (SID). Decreases in plasma water content, for example, decrease hydrogen ion concentration and *vice versa*. Were there a decrease in the amount of water in plasma (Figure 6-22) as the result, for example, of an antidiuretic hormone (ADH) deficiency there would be increased body water loss (polyuria), a water deficit in the extracellular compartment and concentration of strong ions in plasma.

For this example, plasma normally has representatively a strong cation concentration of 146 mEq/L and a strong anion concentration of 104 mEq/L to give a [SID] of 42 mEq/L (i.e. 146-104 = 42). Were there a 20% decrease in plasma water, cation concentration would be increased to 175 mEq/L (i.e.146 + (0.2•146) = 146 + 29 = 175). But anion concentration would be increased only to 125 mEq/L (i.e. 104 + (0.2•104) = 104 + 21 = 125). The new [SID] is 50 mEq/L(i.e. 175-125 = 50). An increase in plasma [SID] (i.e. a more positive [SID]) leads to a non-respiratory alkalemia ( Fencl & Leith, 1993).

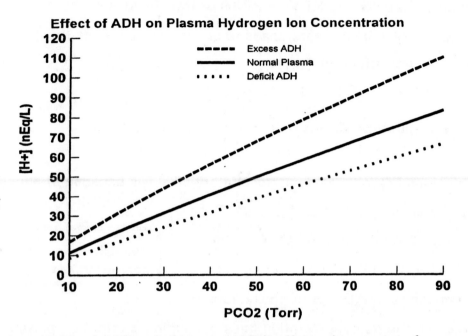

**Figure 6-22:** Antidiuretic hormone (ADH) affects the amount of water in plasma. This reflects on the plasma strong ion difference (SID) to change the solution's hydrogen ion concentration. For example, excess ADH reduces body water loss and increases plasma water, which lowers SID to produce an acidemia. Deficit ADH leads to increased body water loss, increases solute concentration and SID, producing an alkalemia.

Hypochloremia causes an isotonic, ionic imbalance (Fencl & Rossing, 1989). The kidney excretes more chloride than sodium because of "chloride-wasting" diuretics (furosemide, ethacrynic acid, thiazides) or chloride-wasting tubular lesions. It may also result from loss of gastric juice (high [Cl⁻]; Figures 5-16 and 5-18) by vomiting. Gastric juice [SID] is much lower than plasma [SID] (See Chapter 5,Section B.1.3.) which leads to a net positive increase in plasma [SID] and results in alkalemia. Any injected or ingested fluid which increases [Na⁺] relative to [Cl⁻], such as

> Alkalosis and an elevated plasma [SID] are direct consequences of any ingested or injected, material, which increases plasma sodium ion concentration relative to that of plasma chloride ion.

administration of $NaHCO_3$, sodium penicillins or transfusions of blood or blood products containing sodium citrate, leads to an increased plasma [SID] and alkalosis ( Fencl & Leith, 1993;Stewart, 1981).

### D.3.1.2. Non-respiratory Alkalosis Caused by Decreased [Alb]

Hypoalbuminemia produces a non-respiratory alkalosis because of a lower [Alb] producing a lower [Alb⁻] (Chapter 4, Secion C.2.; Rossing et. al., 1986; Fencl & Rossing, 1989; Figge  et. al. 1991,1992). Because inorganic

> Hypoalbuminemia produces a non-respiratory alkalosis.

phosphate concentration ($[P_i]$) is normally  low in plasma, a decrease in its concentration has no significant effect on plasma acid-base status (Fencl & Rossing, 1989; Fencl & Leith, 1993).

### *D.3.2. Non-respiratory Acidosis*

Many types of non-respiratory disorders increase plasma [H⁺] to produce an abnormally low pH.  They arise from either a decrease in plasma [SID], or an increase in plasma non-volatile weak acids, albumin ([Alb]) and inorganic phosphate ($[P_i]$) .  This section describes the effects of changes in [SID] and in [Alb] on non-respiratory acidosis.

### D.3.2.1. Non-Respiratory Acidosis Caused by a Decrease in Plasma [SID]

A decrease in plasma [SID] leads to acidemia.  For example, the "syndrome of inappropriate ADH" (SIADH) is characterized by plasma dilution, reduced  osmolality and

> Acidemia and a lowered plasma [SID] are direct consequences of any mechanisms, which cause the concentration of strong cations to be disproportionately reduced compared to that of strong anions.

hyponatremia. It can be caused from vasopressin (AVP) synthesis, storage and release from tumor tissue, reductions in left atrial filling which stimulates central AVP release, or neurohypophysial release caused by neighboring inflammatory neoplastic or vascular lesions (Streeten, 1987).

A greater-than-normal ADH secretion causes water retention, the voiding of a concentrated urine and dilution of plasma concentrations of strong cations to be disproportionately more than for strong anions. Using the example of a normal plasma sample with a strong cation concentration of 146 mEq/L and a strong anion concentration of 104 mEq/L, the normal [SID] = 42 mEq/L. Were there a 20% increase in plasma water, cation concentration would be decreased to 117 mEq/L (i.e. 146 - 0.2 • 146) = 117 mEq/L. Anion concentration would be decreased to 83 mEq/L (i.e. 104 - 0.2 • 104) = 83 mEq/L. The new [SID] decreased to 34 mEq/L, it became less positive, and caused a non-respiratory acidemia (Fencl & Rossing, 1989; See Section D.3.1.1., Figure 6-22).

[SID] decreases not only by the dilution of strong ions, as in SIADH, but also by an increased concentration of plasma strong anions. For example, loss of colonic fluid, associated with diarrhea, results in a chloride excess in plasma. The hyperchloremia causes [SID] to decrease, producing acidemia. As plasma [Cl⁻] increases, [HCO₃⁻] decreases and the anion gap remains in a normal range (see Section

> Hyperchloremia causes plasma [SID] to decrease (i.e. become less positive) and produces a non-respiratory acidemia

E.1.; Equation 63 or 64) with a hyperchloremic-induced acidosis. The situation is appropriately called a "normal gap acidosis".

Plasma [SID] also decreases because of an increase in strong organic anions. For example, increases in plasma lactate, acetoacetate or β-hydroxybutyrate (ketoacids associated with diabetes), products from metabolizing ethanol, methanol and ethylene glycol, are all strongly dissociated at physiological pH's (See Section

E.5.1.).  They cause [SID] to decrease and

produce an acidosis.  Since these

compounds are all directly associated with

metabolic processes, it is appropriate to

consider the increase they produce in

plasma [$H^+$] to be a "true metabolic

acidosis" (Fencl & Leith, 1993)

> An increase in plasma concentration of acidic products of intermediary metabolism, such as lactate and ketoacids produce a non-respiratory, "true metabolic acidosis".

### D.3.2.2. Non-respiratory Acidosis Caused by Increased [Pi] or [Alb]

Inorganic phosphate concentration ($[P_i]$) is normally low  in plasma (approx. 1

mEq/L). Hyperphosphatemia results from

extensive tissue damage or cell

destruction and inadequate renal

clearance in severe renal failure (Potts,

1987).  Hyperproteinemia, resulting from

> Increased plasma non-volatile weak acids, either due to a hyperalbuminemia or hyperphosphatemia, produces a non-respiratory acidosis.

hemoconcentration, was a major contributor to the acidosis found in patients with

cholera (Wang et. al., 1986).  Both hyperphosphatemia and hyperalbuminemia

cause increased [$P_i^{y-}$] and [$Alb^{x-}$] and a non-respiratory acidosis (Rossing et. al.,

1986; Fencl & Rossing, 1989;Figge et. al., 1991; Chapter 4, Sections C.2. & D.2).

# Section E

## The Anion Gap

## E.1. What is the Anion Gap?

Although all strong cations and anions in plasma  have effects on its acid-base

status, not all are measured in standard clinical tests.  Complete understanding of how any aqueous fluid, including plasma, remains electrically neutral requires that measurements be made of all its cations and all its anions. Were such a complete analysis done, there would be no anion gap. Although the unidentified ions are usually anions,

> The sum of measured anions does not equal the sum of measured cations; the difference is the anion gap.

cations may also be involved. Commonly used electrolyte surveys only analyze serum $[Na^+]$ and $[K^+]$ (approx. 95% of ECF cations), and $[Cl^-]$ and $[HCO_3^-]$ (or total $CO_2$) (approx. 85% of ECF anions) (Emmett & Narins, 1977). The sum of measured anions in such a limited test does not equal the sum of measured cations; the difference, in mEq/L, is the anion gap.

The anion gap (AG) is calculated either as (Abelow,1998; Emmett & Narins,1977; Rose & Post, 2001):

$$AG = [Na^+] - ([Cl^-] + [HCO_3^-]) \qquad (63)$$

or as ( Figge et.al.,1998; Fencl et.al., 2000):

$$AG = ([Na^+] + [K^+]) - ([Cl^-] + [HCO_3^-]) \qquad (64)$$

The anion gap in someone's normal acid-base status is relatively small. It is about 12 mEq/L (range 8-16 mEq/L) when $[K^+]$ is not included in the calculation (Equation 63), and about 16 mEq/L (range 12-20 mEq/L) when it is Equation 64) (Figge et.al.,1998; Emmett & Narins, 1977; Gabow, 1985).

The anion gap, as calculated using Equation 63 is shown by the Gamblegram in Figure 6-23:

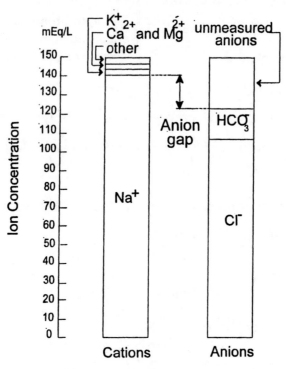

**Figure 6-23:** Anion gap as measured using Equation 63.

The anion gap characterizes a number of physiological and pathophysiological circumstances. Non-respiratory acidosis, for example, results from the accumulation of strong anions (i.e. highly dissociated at plasma pH's) in plasma (Section D.3.2.1.). Increases in plasma lactate and ketoacids, which are strong anions associated with diabetes, produce a so-called, "true" metabolic acidosis. Still other strong anions, such as sulfate, hippurate and urate (associated with renal failure), the ingestion of methyl alcohol (metabolized to formate), ethylene glycol (metabolized to glycolic and oxalic acid) and salicylate intoxication, all result in an increased anion gap.

A low anion gap may develop as the result of an increase in strong cations in plasma, as with the ingestion of lithium products commonly used to control psychiatric disorders, hypercalcemia, and hypermagnesemia , none of which is routinely measured.

> The anion gap  usually represents unmeasured strong anions; less frequently it is created  by unmeasured basic cations.  In all cases, it arises because of incomplete analysis of ion concentrations.

Not all shifts in strong cations and anions in plasma, though, result in an anion gap.  Hyperchloremia, for example, produces a "normal gap acidosis", because the concentration of plasma bicarbonate and chloride ions are reciprocally related and both are routinely measured and used in the calculation of the anion gap (Emmett & Narins, 1977; Figge et.al., 1998).

> Not all shifts in plasma strong cations and anions  produce an anion gap.

In addition, weak non-volatile acids (i.e. albumin and inorganic phosphate) have a strong influence on acid-base state, but are regulated for purposes not directly related to acid-base homeostasis.  These are not routinely measured, but both hyperalbuminemia and hyperphosphatemia are acidic anions and potential causes of non-respiratory acidosis and contribute to an increased anion gap.  On the other hand, hypoalbuminemia  serves as an alkalinizing force which reduces the anion gap and  masks the acidic influence of strongly dissociated anions (Figge et.al., 1998).

## E.2.  Higher-than-normal Anion Gap

The anion gap develops because of increased concentrations of unmeasured strong anions associated with disease, exercise stresses and chemical intoxications.

In diabetes, for example, increases in plasma ketoacids (i.e.$\beta$-hydroxybutyrate and acetoacetate) raise the anion gap to as much as 44 mEq/L (Gabow, 1985) but are usually not measured. Also, an increase in lactate, associated with diabetes or with excessive exercise, increases the anion gap but it's not measured, either. It will also increase because of excessive alcohol or ethylene glycol ingestion, both of which produce strong anions as products of their metabolism. A large anion gap may also reflect the effects of hyperphosphatemia or hyperalbuminemia, weak non-volatile anions, which are not routinely measured but which can contribute to a non-respiratory acidosis (Fencl & Rossing, 1989; Figge et. al., 1991).

## E.3. Normal anion gap

Hyperchloremia typically results from diarrhea, from therapeutic administration of $NH_4Cl$ or from renal failure. Hyperchloremic acidosis results in a so-called "normal anion gap" because of the reciprocal relationship between $[HCO_3^-]$ and $[Cl^-]$ in its calculation (See Equations 63 and 64). Also, a hypoalbuminemia, which alone would decrease the anion gap, could mask the ketoacidosis in a patient with diabetes. The net result would be a "normal anion gap" because of competing unmeasured gap anions ( Figge et. al., 1998).

## E.4. Lower than normal anion gap

A low anion gap, although less common than an increased gap, results from a reduced concentration of unmeasured anions or from retained and unmeasured cations (Emmett & Narins, 1977). For example, hypoalbuminemia is probably the most common cause of a decreased anion gap because albumin's net negative charges represent a significant proportion of the anions in plasma (See Figure 6-24) and of the normal anion gap. Replacement of albumin's unmeasured anions with the measured anions, chloride and bicarbonate, produces a fall in the calculated gap (Emmett & Narins, 1977).

The "syndrome of inappropriate ADH" (SIADH) secretion increases antidiuretic hormone which causes water retention and dilution of plasma electrolytes (See Section D.3.2.1.). In a study of patients with SIADH, 25% had an anion gap of less than 6 mEq/L (Gabow, 1985). IgG paraproteins have isoelectric points higher than 7.40 and therefore are positively charged at normal plasma pH. A significant inverse relationship has been reported between the concentration of IgG paraproteins, having a net positive charge, and the anion gap (Emmett & Narins, 1977). Reduction in the anion gap results from administration of cationic drugs in patients with lithium intoxication as well as those receiving the polycationic antibiotic polymyxin B (Emmett & Narins, 1977; Gabow, 1985).

The anion gap itself does not distinguish among either the unmeasured anions, or cations which cause it. It only indicates that some unmeasured entity is producing the anion deficit. If the acid-base disturbance is a simple non-respiratory acidosis or alkalosis, a thorough history and physical examination gives important clues

> Values for an anion gap are not diagnostic. They indicate only the relative concentrations of electrically charged materials in a solution, which have not been quantified.

about the primary problem. A mixed acid-base disorder, as for example a chronic respiratory acidosis combined with an inadequate or inappropriate compensation by the kidneys, adds a non-respiratory acidosis to the initiating respiratory acidosis. Two or more factors could contribute to a non-respiratory acidosis, such as lactate accumulation due to inadequate perfusion complicating diabetic ketoacidosis.

## E.5.  An HION Alternative to the Anion Gap

Electroneutrality requires that in plasma, as in all other body fluids, cation concentrations must equal anion concentrations. This principle is important in the development of the HION concepts and forms the basis for not considering hydrogen ion in isolation, but rather with all other ions in body solutions (Stewart, 1981). Common analyses and interpretations of acid-base physiology make limited use of ion measurements, either those represented in the Henderson-Hasselbalch equation or those with the anion gap.

Chapters 2 to 5 stressed the importance of four independent variables, as well as water, the universal solvent, for determining the concentrations of dependent variables in biological solutions. The independent variable $PCO_2$, is responsible for determining the concentrations of all of the dependent variables represented in the Henderson-Hasselbalch equation (i.e. $H^+$ and $HCO_3^-$ or total $CO_2$), in addition to several others, either directly or indirectly (i.e. $CO_3^{2-}$, $OH^-$ ;Chapter 3). The independent variable [SID], consists of several inorganic ions (i.e. $Na^+$, $K^+$, $Ca^{2+}$, $Mg^{2+}$ and $Cl^-$ ;Chapter 2), which play a role in governing the concentrations of all the dependent variables. The independent variable $[A_{TOT}]$ was identified with two ionic species (i.e. $Alb^{x-}$ and $P_i^{y-}$) associated with the net negative charges on plasma albumin and inorganic phosphate, respectively (Chapter 4).

Equations developed here provide a more complete analysis of factors contributing to the anion gap than are those commonly presented elsewhere. Some incorporate materials which are routinely measured, namely $PCO_2$, pH, and [Albumin] (g/dL), total $[P_i]$ (mM or mg/dl phosphorus) (Chapter 4, Sections C.2. & D.2.). Direct determination of [SID] is impractical, but it can be derived (Figge,1992).

### E.5.1. Effective SID

The strong ion difference ([SID]) is defined in Chapter 2 as the difference between the sum of strong cations, which are readily identified and analyzed (i.e. $Na^+$, $K^+$, $Ca^{2+}$, $Mg^{2+}$) and the lone strong anion, $Cl^-$. This difference in concentrations is called an "inorganic [SID]" (Stewart, 1981), or an "apparent [SID]" ($[SID]_a$) (Figge et. al., 1992):

$$[SID]_a = ([Na^+] + [K^+] + [Ca^{2+}] + [Mg^{2+}]) - [Cl^-] \qquad (65)$$

In all body fluids, including plasma, there are always some anions ($[XA^-]$) which are either unidentified, or not routinely analyzed, as in the anion gap. All of them are acidic and are associated either with disease processes or with renal failure (i.e. lactate, sulphate, ketoacids, salicylate). They are strongly dissociated at physiological pH's. They are associated with [SID] along with the strongly dissociated ions shown in Equation 65.

"Effective SID" ($[SID]_e$) is defined as:

$$[SID]_e = ([Na^+] + [K^+] + [Ca^{2+}] + [Mg^{2+}]) - [Cl^-] - [XA^-] \qquad (66)$$

Combining Equations 65 and 66, defines the concentration of unidentified strong anions, as:

$$[XA^-] = [SID]_a - [SID]_e \qquad (67)$$

Effective SID ($[SID]_e$) is calculated, if all the remaining independent variables and pH are known (i.e. $PCO_2$, $[SID]_a$ , [Alb] and $[P_i]$). Electrical neutrality in plasma is expressed as:

$$[SID]_e + [H^+] = [OH^-] + [HCO_3^-] + [CO_3^{2-}] + [Alb^{x-}] + [P_i^{y-}] \tag{68}$$

Because [$H^+$], [$OH^-$], [$CO_3^{2-}$]) are negligibly small in plasma:

$$[SID]_e = [HCO_3^-] + [Alb^{x-}] + [P_i^{y-}] \tag{69}$$

and shown in Figure 6-24:

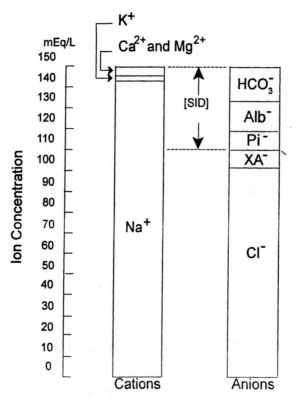

**Figure 6-24:** Plasma effective [SID] ($[SID]_e$) is calculated as the sum of $[HCO_3^-]$, $[Alb^x]$ and $[P_i^y]$,( Equation 71).

Because [$HCO_3^-$] is determined from pH and $PCO_2$ (Chapter 3, Equation 22):

$$[HCO_3^-] = 1000 \cdot K_c \cdot \frac{PCO_2}{10^{-pH}} \tag{70}$$

where:

$K_c = 2.46 \cdot 10^{-11}$ (Eq/L)$^2$ • Torr$^{-1}$ @37°C

$PCO_2$ = partial pressure of $CO_2$ (Torr)

$10^{-pH}$ = [H$^+$] Eq/L

1000 = factor which converts from Eq/L to mEq/L

Combining Equation 46 (for calculating [Alb$^x$ ]), and Equation 60 (for calculating [P$_i^y$ ]) with Equation 70 shows that (Figge et. al.,1992):

$$[SID]_e = 1000 \cdot K_c \cdot \frac{PCO_2}{10^{-pH}} + 10 \cdot [Alb] \cdot (0.123 \cdot pH - 0.631) \\ +[P_i] \cdot (0.309 \cdot pH - 0.469) \tag{71}$$

where:

[SID]$_e$ has units of mEq/L

[Alb] has units of g/dL

[P$_i$] has units of mmol/L

Equation 71 demonstrates the effects of three independent variables (i.e. $PCO_2$, [Alb] and [P$_i$]), and the dependent variable, pH for calculating

> The analyses for calculating an effective [SID] provide a more complete ionic profile than when only factors in the Henderson-Hasselbalch and anion gap equations are evaluated.

an effective SID ($[SID]_e$). The anion gap is typically expressed on the basis of clinical measurements of sodium, chloride and bicarbonate ions. Equation 71 shows how anions that are not routinely measured also contribute to an effective SID ($[SID]_e$ ). Information about $[SID]_e$ (Equation 71) and $[SID]_a$ (Equation 65) gives a rational basis for diagnosis and treatment of acidemia. Such analyses provide a nearly complete ionic profile for acid-base status, which is considerably more complete than when only factors in the Henderson-Hasselbalch equation are evaluated.

### E.5.2. Correcting the Anion Gap for Abnormal Serum [Alb]

The plasma anion gap is a long-standing diagnostic tool used in the evaluation of non-respiratory ("metabolic") acidosis. It was originally used to differentiate hyperchloremic acidosis, where the gap was normal, from gap acidoses for which the anion gap was increased above normal. The observed anion gap, however, is often unreliable in identifying increased gap anions (Emmet & Narins, 1977;Gabow, 1985; Fencl & Rossing, 1989). Hypoalbuminemia, for example, a disturbance often seen in hospitalized patients (Emmett & Narins, 1977), particularly those in critical care, ( Fencl & Rossing, 1989; Rossing et. al., 1986) can mask an increase in gap anions by lowering the value of the anion gap ( Emmett & Narins, 1977; Gabow,1985; Rossing et. al, 1986).

A detailed analysis of acid-base data including serum electrolytes and albumin concentrations, was used to derive a correction factor which adjusts the observed anion gap, calculated by Equation 64, for low concentrations of serum albumin (Figge et. al., 1998). This correction then reveals whether an increase in gap anions was present.

A   general statement of electrical neutrality in plasma (mEq/L) is:

$$[Na^+] + [K^+] + [Ca^{2+}] + [Mg^{2+}] + [H^+] - [OH^-] - [HCO_3^-] - [CO_3^{2-}]$$
$$- [Cl^-] - [Alb^{x-}] - [P_i^{y-}] - [XA^-] = 0 \tag{72}$$

Because $H^+$, $OH^-$ and $CO_3^{2-}$ concentrations are in nEq/L and μEq/L, their contributions to electrical neutrality are negligible and they are not evaluated. The equation for electrical neutrality is then:

$$([Na^+] + [K^+] - [Cl^-] - [HCO_3^-]) - ([XA^-] + [P_i^{y-}]) =$$
$$[Alb^{x-}] - [Ca^{2+}] - [Mg^{2+}] \tag{73}$$

The concentrations for $Na^+$, $K^+$, $Cl^-$ and $HCO_3^-$ represent the anion gap (AG; See Equation 64). The concentrations $[XA^-]$ and $[P_i^{y-}]$ define the total concentration of gap anions (i.e. all anions other than $Cl^-$, $HCO_3^-$ and $Alb^{x-}$; $[GA^-] = [XA^-] + [P_i^{y-}]$).

Then,

$$AG - [GA^-] = [Alb^{x-}] - [Ca^{2+}] - [Mg^{2+}] \tag{74}$$

To derive $AG - [GA^-]$, it is necessary to measure $[Ca^{2+}]$ and $[Mg^{2+}]$, and to calculate $[Alb^{x-}]$ as a function of $[Alb]$ and pH (Equation 46; Figge et. al., 1992). To calculate the anion gap (AG), it is necessary to measure $[Na^+]$, $[K^+]$ and $[Cl^-]$ and calculate $[HCO_3^-]$ using Equation 70. AG - $[GA^-]$ was a linear function of [Alb] in g/dL (Figge, et. al.1998) so that:

$$AdjustedAG = ObservedAG + 2.5 \cdot (Normal[Alb] - Observed[Alb]) \qquad (75)$$

where:

AG = anion gap

[Alb] = albumin concentration in g/dL

2.5 = Slope of the line relating (AG - $[GA^-]$; mEq/L) to ([Alb]; g/dL)

The ratio of $\Delta$(AG - $[GA^-]$;mEq/L) to $\Delta$([Alb]; g/dL) agrees with that used to correct the anion gap when albumin concentration is low (Gabow. 1985; Rose & Post, 2001).

## E.6. What It All Means

Many physiology textbooks have for years evaluated acid-base relationships solely on the basis of the Henderson-Hasselbalch equation. It is hard to find any that don't. An attraction for doing this is largely because of its simplicity. It shows just three variables, $PCO_2$, $[HCO_3^-]$ and pH, only two of which need to be measured in order to calculate the third, which is often $[HCO_3^-]$. Although this is a simple enough calculation, it does not provide adequate accuracy, or detail, for many purposes, including the needs of most physicians. It is further misleading in that many times a blood sample's [total $CO_2$] is measured, as with a Sequential Multichannel Autoanalyzer (SMA), then erroneously presumed to be equal to its $[HCO_3^-]$. The trade-off between simplicity and accuracy often leads to misinterpretations.

To provide more complete analyses, clinical assessments typically include the anion gap requiring two additional measurements, those for the major cation, $[Na^+]$ and $[Cl^-]$, which when combined with $[HCO_3^-]$, form the two major anions . The concept of the anion gap rose from concepts revealed in a Gamblegram and is based on the required electrical neutrality of serum (Gabow, 1985). This is useful to distinguish an elevated anion gap, which is considered to be synonymous with a non-respiratory (so-called, "metabolic") acidosis, from, for example, a hyperchloremic acidosis which is characterized by a normal anion gap (Emmett & Narins, 1977).

Although the anion gap is useful for detecting the effects of electrolytes, which are not normally measured, it is not specific.   Also, were the anion gap normal, or lower than normal, caused, for example by hypoalbuminemia, the

> More detailed assessments are required to provide a more complete ionic profile for analyzing plasma acid-base status.

alkalinizing effect it produces could mask acidifying effects of strong anions, such as the keto acids and lactate (Figge et al., 1998).  More detailed assessments are necessary to provide a more complete ionic profile for analyzing plasma acid-base status.

Blood  plasma (or serum) is most commonly analyzed clinically, because samples are easily collected and its composition gives important diagnostic information.  Its composition reflects the body's extracellular fluid compartment and defines  whole body acid-base status. Although just the components of the anion gap and Henderson- Hasselbalch calculations have been used for many years in diagnosis of acid-base disorders, the principles on which they are based and the justification for their use has been either forgotten, or ignored.

For example, the anion gap is based on the concept of electrical neutrality of plasma and serum. It gives a clinical short-cut for an estimate of electrical neutrality (Emmett & Narins, 1977; Gabow, 1985). To document electrical neutrality, however, requires many more measurements than are in either Equation 63, or 64. Sodium and potassium account for 95% of all cations and chloride and bicarbonate account for approximately 85% of ECF anions (Emmett & Narins, 1977). Considering other unmeasured cations and anions, some strongly dissociated and others only partially dissociated it is not surprising that the anion gap lacks specificity and precision, and represents the difference between unmeasured anions and cations (Rose & Post, 2001).

Equations developed in Sections E.5.1. (Figge et. al., 1992) expand the definition of the strong ion difference and appropriately account for the effect of many of the strong anions ([XA$^-$]) encountered in disease processes contributing to non-respiratory acidosis (i.e. ketoacids, lactate and metabolic end-products of ingested poisons). Many of them, although not directly measured, contribute to an increased [SID] and in some cases can be identified from a complete patient history . The calculation of an effective [SID] (i.e. Equations 69 & 71; Figure 6-24) offers insight into the dependent variables and weakly dissociated anions (i.e. [HCO$_3^-$], [P$_i^{y-}$] and [Alb$^{x-}$]), which affect the anion gap.

> Calculation of an effective [SID] offers insight into the dependent variables which affect the anion gap.

Bicarbonate is shown to have a reciprocal relationship with chloride in the usual anion gap calculation (Equations 63 & 64). Inorganic phosphate and albumin contribute to the anion gap. For example, hyperalbuminemia and hyperphosphatemia increase it (Section E.2.), and hypoalbuminemia decreases it (Section E.4.). The calculation of effective [SID] in plasma includes not only the chloride ion, but also strong anions, $XA^-$'s, associated with disease processes, which contribute to a non-respiratory acidosis.

Equations in Section E.5.2. were developed specifically to correct the usual anion gap calculation for the influence of abnormal concentrations of albumin in plasma (Figge et. al, 1991, 1998). The observed anion gap was often found to be less reliable for finding increased concentrations of gap anions, particularly in critically ill patients with hypoalbuminemia than when the effect of albumin was also evaluated (McAuliffe et. al.,1986; Fencl & Rossing, 1989).

Calculating the anion gap (AG) using Equation 63 provides a less reliable prediction of the data relating (AG - [$GA^-$]; mEq/L) to (serum [Alb]; g/dL) than when Equation 64 is used. Both methods, however, show there is a dependence of the observed anion gap on the serum albumin concentration. These data (Figge et. al.,1998) come from 265 measurements from 152 patients in an intensive care

> Serum allbumin concentration measurements are important in routine examinations, especially for the critically ill.

unit. Forty-nine percent of them had serum albumin concentrations of less than 20 g/L (compared to 44 g/L in normal subjects). This shows the importance of albumin concentration measurements in routine examinations, especially for the critically ill.

Table 6.7 uses HION principles in the diagnosis of acid-base disturbances based on measurements in blood plasma. Data for $PCO_2$, [SID], [Alb] and [$P_i$], provide a rational basis for detecting the cause of simple, as well as more complex, mixed acid-base imbalances.

| Table 6-7 Plasma Acid-Base Abnormalities* | | |
|---|---|---|
| **Cause** | **Condition** | |
| | *acidemia* | *alkalemia* |
| Respiratory | hypercapnia | hypocapnia |
| Non-respiratory ("metabolic") | hyperalbuminemia hyperphosphatemia | hypoalbuminemia |
| | [SID] becomes: | |
| | less positive by: ✔ water dilution ✔ hyperchloremia ✔ strong anions | more positive by: ✔ water conc. ✔ hypochloremia ✔ hypernatremia |

*Adapted from Fencl & Leith, 1993

The independent variable, $PaCO_2$, is the primary cause of a respiratory acid-base disorder. Hypoventilation of the lung's alveoli causes $PaCO_2$ to increase resulting in an acidemia in systemic arterial blood. Hyperventilation causes $PaCO_2$ to decrease resulting in an alkalemia.

The independent variable, [SID], is a primary cause of a non-respiratory acid-base disorder. It is normally positive in most biological fluids, including plasma. When it becomes less positive in blood plasma, it causes a non-respiratory acidemia . Metabolic, gastrointestinal and renal mechanisms cause a reduction in plasma [SID] (See Section D.3.2.1.). When [SID] becomes more positive in blood plasma, it causes a non-respiratory alkalemia (See Section D.3.1.1.).

Two non-volatile weak acids in plasma, albumin ([Alb]) and inorganic phosphate ($[P_i]$) (See Chapter 4, Sections C & D), are also independent variables. An increased concentration of both albumin and inorganic phosphate leads to an increase in the concentration of their ionized forms, $Alb^{x-}$ and $P_i^{y-}$, both of which are also functions of pH or $[H^+]$. Since they are plasma anions, the excess total concentration produces an acidemia (See Section D.3.2.2.). Inorganic phosphate concentration is normally low in plasma, so that further reductions have little effect on acid-base status. Reductions below normal in plasma [Alb], however, result in a non-respiratory alkalemia (See Section D.3.1.2.), reducing the anion gap, and masking a non-respiratory acidosis ( See Section E.5.2.).

Table 6-7 summarizes the primary abnormalities of the four independent variables in blood plasma that produce respiratory and non-respiratory acid-base disturbances. For such analysis, it is necessary to quantify the molecular and ionic composition of plasma. For example, sodium, potassium, calcium, magnesium, phosphorus, albumin and chloride concentrations are routinely measured to document and complement an annual physical examination. All necessary data are available to assess any abnormalities in independent variables when additional information about arterial pH and $PCO_2$ is also collected.

## E.7. Background for HION Concepts

HION concepts arise predominantly from data in three publications (Stewart, 1978, 1981 & 1983). They rest firmly on physical chemical principles governing ionic composition of all aqueous solutions, including body fluids. Data supporting HION concepts apply in the diagnosis of clinical disorders of acid-base balance using the collective term, $[A_{TOT}]$, to represent the weak, non-volatile acids in plasma (Jones, 1987, 1990 & 1997).

The "Fencl group" in the 1990s expanded many earlier observations (Van Slyke, 1928; Sendroy & Hastings, 1927; Emmett & Narins, 1977) of acid-base phenomena involving the contributions of the weak, non-volatile acids (Figge et. al., 1991, 1992, 1998; see also Reeves, 1991). Their research provided more precise and complete quantification for analyses available earlier in the twentieth century (Astrup & Severinghaus, 1986; Davenport, 1974; Siggaard-Andersen, 1974) and still used today. A recent report provides calculations and a computer program (Fencl et. al., 2000) to make detailed analyses of clinical laboratory data for diagnosing metabolic acid-base disturbances. A supplement shows why two currently used methods relying on plasma bicarbonate concentration and the anion gap or on "base-excess" did not reliably diagnose metabolic acid-base disturbances in critically ill patients (Fencl et. al., 2000).

An alternative way has been proposed (Watson, 1999) of including [Alb] and $[P_i]$ as a substitute for $[A_{TOT}]$ in plasma (See Chapter 4, Equation 42), using data on albumin's amino acid side chains (Figge et. al., 1991, 1992). In the pH range 6.8 to 7.8 albumin contains approximately 99 amino acid side chains with nearly fixed negative charge (mainly aspartic and glutamic acid) and approximately 77 groups with nearly fixed positive charge (mainly arginine and lysine), as suggested earlier (Reeves, 1997). There are 16 histidine residues on albumin (Figge et. al., 1991) and the imidazole group reacts with hydrogen ion in a slightly different manner than described in Chapter 4, Section A, so that the mass balance equation, corresponding to Equation 39 is:

$$[AH^+] = \frac{[H^+] \cdot [A_H TOT]}{(K_H + [H^+])} \qquad (76)$$

where:

  $[AH^+]$ = the positively charged histidine imidazole group

  $[A_H TOT]$ = the concentration of histidine residues in albumin

   = [Alb] • 10 • 16/66,500, and [Alb] is in g/dL

   16 = number of histidine residues/mole albumin

   66,500 = molecular weight of albumin

$K_H$ = the average dissociation constant for histidine's imidazole group
= $1.77 \cdot 10^{-7}$ Eq/L @ 37.5 °C (Reeves, 1976)

and the final substitution for [A⁻], the net charge on serum albumin is:

$$[A^-] = [A_{fixed}^-] - \frac{[H^+] \cdot [A_H TOT]}{(K_H + [H^+])} \tag{77}$$

where:

$[A_{fixed}^-]$ = [Alb] • 10 • 21/66,500, and [Alb] is in g/dL

21 = number of net negative charges per mole of albumin

66,500 = molecular weight of albumin

Rather than use all three of the dissociations (factor Z; Figge et al.,1991, 1992) to account for the other weak non-volatile acid in plasma, [$P_i$], two of them have pK values far removed from the physiological pH range, and the phosphate contribution to charge becomes (Watson, 1999):

$$[P_i^-] = [P_i] \cdot \frac{(2 - [H^+])}{(K_2 + [H^+])} \tag{78}$$

where:

$[P_i^-]$ = the ionized form of inorganic phosphate

$[P_i]$ = the total concentration of inorganic phosphate in plasma

$K_2$ = the second ionization constant of phosphate, $2.17 \cdot 10^{-7}$ moles/L
@ 37°C

Equations 77 and 78 are incorporated in Equation 41 (Chapter 4), the equation for electrical neutrality, as substitutes for the last item to the left of the equal sign. A computer program incorporating this equation allows for calculation of concentrations of the dependent variables (Watson, 1999).

The three slightly different approaches for extending and testing Stewart's original quantitative approach to understanding acid-base chemistry represent the latest developments in this field. HION concepts have been in the scientific literature for many years, but have often been forgotten, misinterpreted or misused. Some HION concepts involve complex equations and calculations that were impractical and were rejected. This resulted in simpler solutions and short-cut methods which are still found in basic physiological as well as clinical textbooks. Use of better analytical tools, more rigorous analysis of physical chemical concepts and use of computer solutions of analytical data have put acid-base chemistry on a firm and logical foundation.

# Section F

## Main Points from Chapter 6

✔   The Henderson-Hasselbalch equation in combination with the Anion Gap
    calculation fail to provide a complete analysis of acid-base disorders.

✔   HION concepts promote use of more routine analyses which allow for a more
    complete definition and diagnosis of acid-base disorders.

✔   Acid-base disorders originating in the respiratory system are characterized by
    abnormal values of $PaCO_2$.  Increased systemic arterial $PCO_2$ (hypercapnia)
    produces an acidemia and respiratory acidosis.  Hypocapnia (decreased
    systemic arterial $PCO_2$) produces an alkalemia and respiratory alkalosis.

✔   Non-respiratory (so-called metabolic) acid-base disorders are characterized by
    abnormal values of plasma [SID] and/or of plasma's non-volatile weak acids,
    albumin ([Alb]) and inorganic phosphate ($[P_i]$).

✔   The concentration of plasma strong cations is greater than the concentration
    of strong anions and plasma [SID] is normally positive. Anything causing
    plasma [SID] to decrease causes an acidemia and a non-respiratory acidosis.
    Anything causing plasma [SID] to increase (i.e. become more positive) causes
    an alkalemia and a non-respiratory alkalosis.

✔ Both an increased concentration of serum albumin ([Alb]; hyperalbuminemia) and inorganic phosphate ([$P_i$]; hyperphosphatemia) will cause an acidemia and a non-respiratory acidosis. A decreased concentration of serum albumin (hypoalbuminemia) causes an alkalemia and non-respiratory alkalosis. Serum phosphate concentration is normally low and a decrease in its concentration has an insignificant effect on acid-base status.

✔ The respiratory system can compensate for non-respiratory disturbances by adjustments in $PaCO_2$. A non-respiratory acidosis is compensated by hyperventilation and a reduction in $PaCO_2$. A non-respiratory alkalosis is compensated by hypoventilation and a rise in $PaCO_2$. Respiratory adjustments are rapid and plasma [$H^+$] returns toward its normal value of 7.40. Compensations are never complete.

✔ The kidneys can compensate for respiratory disturbances by adjustments in extracellular [SID]. A respiratory acidosis is compensated by excretion of chloride ions, in excess of sodium ions in the urine and reducing plasma [SID]. A respiratory alkalosis is compensated by renal retention of chloride ions, and lowering plasma [SID].

# REFERENCES

1.    Abelow, B.:*Understanding Acid-Base.*  Williams & Wilkins, Baltimore, MD,1998.

2.    Adams, G.R., Foley, J.M. and Meyer, R.A.: Muscle buffer capacity estimated from pH changes during rest-to-work transitions.  J. Appl. Physiol. 69: 968-972, 1990.

3.    Astrup, P. and Severinghaus, J.W.: *The History of Blood Gases, Acids and Bases* Radiometer A/S, Munksgaard International Publishers, Copenhagen, 1986.

4.    Braunwald, E., Isselbacher, K.J., Petersdorf, R.G., Wilson, J.D., Martin, J.B. and Fauci, A.S., editors: *Harrison's Principles of Internal Medicine*, 11th edition, McGraw-Hill Book Co. ,New York, NY,1987.

5.    Buchan, A.M.J.: Digestion and Absorption, Chapter 73 in *Textbook of Physiology*, Vol. 2, 21st edition, ed. by Patton, H.D., Fuchs, A.F., Hille, B., Scher, A.M. and Steiner, R., W.B. Saunders Co., Philadelphia, PA, 1989.

6.    Burtis, C.A. and Ashwood, E.R., editors: *Tietz Textbook of Clinical Chemistry*, 3rd edition, W.B. Saunders Co., Philadelphia, PA, 1999

7.    Chinard, F.P.: Introductory remarks: An elementary approach to the carbon dioxide system.  In: *Current Concepts of Acid-Base Measurement*, ed. by H.E. Whipple, Annals of the New York Academy of Sciences 133 (Article 1):87-89, 1966.

8.  Cohen, J.J. and Kassirer, J.P.: *Acid-Base*, Little, Brown and Co.Inc., Boston, MA, 1982.

9.  Davenport, H. W.: *The ABC of Acid-Base Chemistry*, 6th edition, The University of Chicago Press, Chicago, IL, 1974.

10. Davenport, H. W.: *Physiology of the Digestive Tract: An Introductory Text.* 4th edition, Year Book Medical Publishers, Inc., Chicago, IL, 1977.

11. Davis, B.D.: On the importance of being ionized.  Archiv. Biochem. and Biophys.  78: 497-509, 1958.

12. Emmett, M. and Narins, R.G.: Clinical use of the anion gap.  Medicine (Baltimore) 56: 38-54, 1977.

13. Fencl, V., Jabor, A., Kazda, A. and Figge, J.: Diagnosis of metabolic acid-base disturbances in critically ill patients.  Am. J. Respir. Crit. Care Med. 162: 2246-2251, 2000.

14. Fencl, V. and Leith, D.E.: Stewart's quantitative acid-base chemistry: Applications in biology and medicine.  Respiration Physiology 91: 1-16, 1993.

15. Fencl, V. and Rossing, T.H.: Acid-base disorders in critical care medicine. Ann.Rev.Medicine 40:17-29, 1989.

16. Figge, J. , Rossing, T.H. and Fencl, V.: The role of serum proteins in acid-base equilibria. J. Lab. Clin. Med. 117: 453-467, 1991.

17. Figge, J., Mydosh,T. and Fencl, V.: Serum proteins and acid-base equilibria: a follow-up. J. Lab. Clin. Med. 120: 713-719, 1992.

18. Figge, J., Jabor, A., Kazda, A., and Fencl, V.: Anion gap and hypoalbuminemia. Critical Care Medicine 26: 1807-1810, 1998.

19. Forte, J.G. and Wolosin, J.M.: HCl Secretion by the Gastric Oxyntic Cell, Chapter 27 in *Physiology of the Gastrointestinal Tract*, 2nd edition, Vol. 1, Johnson, L.R., Editor-in-Chief, Raven Press, New York, NY, 1987.

20. Gabow, P.A.: Disorders associated with an altered anion gap. Kidney International 27: 472-483, 1985.

21. Gamble, J.L.: *Chemical Anatomy Physiology and Pathology of Extracellular Fluid; A Lecture Syllabus*, 5th edition, Harvard University Press, Cambridge, MA, 1952.

22. Gamble, J.L., Ross, G.S. and Tisdall, F.F.: The metabolism of fixed base during fasting. J. Biol. Chem. 57: 633-695, 1923.

23. Ganong, W.F.: *Review of Medical Physiology.* 18th edition, Appleton and Lange, Stamford, CT, 1997.

24. Guyton, A.C. and Hall, J.E.: Secretory functions of the alimentary tract, Chapter 64 in *Textbook of Medical Physiology,* 9th edition, W.B. Saunders Company, Philadelphia, PA, 1996.

25.  Harned, H.S. and Owen, B.B.: *The Physical Chemistry of Electrolytic Solutions.* 3$^{rd}$ edition, Reinhold, New York, 1958.

26.  Harvey, A. M.: Classics in Clinical Science: James L. Gamble and "Gamblegrams". Amer. Jour.Medicine 66: 904-906, 1979.

27.  Henderson, L.J.: *Blood, A Study in General Physiology.* Yale University Press, New Haven,CT, 1928.

28.  Hendrix, T.R.: The secretory function of the alimentary canal, Chapter 54 in *Medical Physiology,* 14$^{th}$ ed., Vol. 2, ed. by V.B. Mountcastle, C.V. Mosby Co., St. Louis, 1980.

29.  Holick, M.F., Krane, S.M. and Potts, J.T., Jr.:Calcium, phosphorus and bone metabolism: calcium-regulating hormones, Chapter 335 in *Harrison's Principles of Internal Medicine,* 11$^{th}$ edition, ed. by Braunwald, E., Isselbacher, K.J., Petersdorf, R.G., Wilson, J.D., Martin, J.B. and Fauci, A.S., McGraw-Hill Book Co., New York, NY, 1987.

30.  Hootman, S.R. and Williams, J.A.: Stimulus-Secretion Coupling in the Pancreatic Acinus, Chapter 41 in *Physiology of the Gastrointestinal Tract*, 2$^{nd}$ edition, Vol. 2, L.R. Johnson, Editor-in-Chief, Raven Press, New York, NY, 1987.

31.  Jones, N.L.: *Blood Gases and Acid-Base Physiology,* 2$^{nd}$ edition, Thieme Medical Publishers, Inc., New York, NY, 1987.

32. Jones, N.L.: A quantitative physicochemical approach to acid-base physiology. Clin. Biochem. 23:189-195, 1990.

33. Jones, N.L.: Acid-Base Physiology. In: *The Lung: Scientific Foundations*, Vol. 2, Chapter 123 ed. by Crystal,R.G., West,J.W., et al., Lippincott-Raven Publishers, Philadelphia, PA, 1997.

34. Kutchai, H.C.: Gastrointestinal Secretions, Chapter 38 in *Physiology,* 4th edition, edited by Berne, R.M. and Levy, M.N., Mosby, Inc., St. Louis, MO, 1998.

35. McAuliffe, J.J., Lind, L.J., Leith, D.E. and Fencl, V.: Hypoproteinemic alkalosis. Am. J. Med. 81: 86-90, 1986.

36. McGuigan, J.E.: Peptic Ulcer, Chapter 235 in *Harrison's Principles of Internal Medicine,* 11th edition, ed. by Braunwald, E., Isselbacher, K.J., Petersdorf, R.G.,Wilson, J.D., Martin, J.B. and Fauci, A.S., McGraw-Hill Book Co., New York, NY, 1987.

37. Petersen, O.H.: Electrophysiology of Exocrine Gland Cells, Chapter 24 in *Physiology of the Gastrointestinal Tract,* 2nd edition, Vol. 2, L.R. Johnson, Editor-in-Chief, Raven Press, New York, NY, 1987.

38. Potts, J.T., Jr.: Diseases of the parathyroid gland and other hyper- and hypocalcemic disorders, Chapter 336 in *Harrison's Principles of Internal Medicine,* 11th edition, ed. by Braunwald, E., Isselbacher, K.J., Petersdorf, R.G.,Wilson, J.D., Martin, J.B. and Fauci, A.S., McGraw-Hill Book Co., New York, NY, 1987.

39. Rahn, H.: Introduction and general concepts. In: *Acid-Base Regulation and Body Temperature*, ed. by Rahn, H. and Prakash,O., Martinus Nijhoff, Boston, MA, 1985.

40. Rahn, H and Howell, B.J.: The $OH^-/H^+$ concept of acid-base balance: historical development. Respir. Physiol. 33: 91-97, 1978

41. Rahn, H., Reeves, R.B.,and Howell, B.J.: Hydrogen ion regulation, temperature and evolution. Am. Rev. of Resp. Disease 112: 165-172, 1975.

42. Reeves, R.B.:Temperature-induced changes in blood acid-base status: pH and $PCO_2$ in a binary buffer. J. Appl. Physiol. 40: 752-761, 1976.

43. Reeves, R.B.: What are normal acid-base conditions in man when body temperature changes? In: *Acid-Base Regulation and Body Temperature*, ed. by Rahn, H. and Prakash,O., Martinus Nijhoff, Boston, MA, 1985.

44. Reeves, R.B.: Error proved and corrected: Net anionic charge on serum albumin. J. Lab. Clin. Med. 117:437, 1991.

45. Reeves, R.B.: Acid-Base Balance in hypothermia. Chap. 214 in *The Lung*: *Scientific Foundations*, 2nd edition, ed. by Crystal,R.G., West,J.B., et.al., Lippincott-Raven Publishers, Philadelphia, PA, 1997.

46. Rose, B.D.and Post, T.W.: *Clinical Physiology of Acid-Base and Electrolyte Disorders*, 5th edition, McGraw-Hill, Inc., New York, NY, 2001.

47.   Rossing, T.H., Maffeo, N. and Fencl, V.: Acid-base effects of altering plasma protein concentration in human blood in vitro.  J. Appl. Physiol. 61: 2260-2265, 1986.

48.   Sachs, G.:The Gastric Proton Pump: The $H^+$,$K^+$-ATPase, Chapter 28 in *Physiology of the Gastrointestinal Tract*, $2^{nd}$ edition, Vol. 1, L.R. Johnson, Editor-in-Chief, Raven Press, New York, NY, 1987.

49.   Schulz, I.: Electrolyte and Fluid Secretion in the Exocrine Pancreas, Chapter 42 in *Physiology of the Gastrointestinal Tract*, $2^{nd}$ edition, Vol. 2, L.R. Johnson, Editor-in-Chief, Raven Press, New York, NY, 1987.

50.   Sendroy, J. Jr. and Hastings, A.B.: Studies of the solubility of calcium salts. II. The solubility of tertiary calcium phosphate in salt solutions and biological fluids.  J. Biol. Chem. 71: 783-796, 1927.

51.   Siggaard-Andersen, O.: *The Acid-Base Status of Blood*, $4^{th}$ edition, Williams & Wilkins Co., Baltimore, MD, 1974, 229p.

52.   Stewart, P.A.: Independent and dependent variables of acid-base control. Respir. Physiol. 33: 9-26, 1978.

53.   Stewart, P.A.: *How to Understand Acid-Base: A Quantitative Acid-Base Primer for Biology and Medicine,* Elsevier North Holland, Inc., NY, 1981.

54.   Stewart, P.A.: Modern quantitative acid-base chemistry.  Canadian J. Physiol. and Pharmacol. 61:1444-1461, 1983.

55. Streeten, D.H.P., Moses, A.M. and Miller, M: Disorders of the Neurohypophysis, Chapter 323 in *Harrison's Principles of Internal Medicine*, 11th edition, ed. by Braunwald, E., Isselbacher, K.J., Petersdorf,R.G., Wilson, J.D., Martin, J.B. and Fauci, A.S., McGraw-Hill Book Co., New York, NY, 1987.

56. Swan, H.: Acid-base management during hypothermic circulatory arrest for cardiac surgery. In: *Acid-Base Regulation and Body Temperature,* ed. by Rahn, H. and Prakash,O., Martinus Nijhoff, Boston, MA, 1985.

57. Tanner, G.A.: Acid-Base Balance  Chapter 25 in *Medical Physiology*, edited by Rhoades, R. A. and Tanner, G.A., Little, Brown and Company, Boston, MA, 1995.

58. Tso, P.: Gastrointestinal Secretion, Chapter 28 in *Medical Physiology*, edited by Rhoades, R. A. and Tanner, G.A., Little, Brown and Company, Boston, MA, 1995.

59. Van Leeuwen, A.M.: Net cation equivalency ('base binding power') of the plasma proteins. Acta Med. Scand. 176 (Suppl. 422): 1-212, 1964.

60. Van Slyke, D.D., Hastings, A.B., Hiller, A. and Sendroy, J., Jr.: Studies of gas and electrolyte equilibria in blood.  XIV. The amounts of alkali bound by serum albumin and globulin.  J. Biol. Chem. 79: 769-780, 1928.

61.  Wang, F., Butler, T., Rabbani, G.H., and Jones, P.K.: The acidosis of cholera: contributions of hyperproteinemia, lactic acidemia, and hyperphosphatemia to an increased serum anion gap. New England Jour. of Medicine 315: 1591-1595, 1986.

62.  Watson, P.D.: Modeling the effects of proteins on pH in plasma. J. Appl. Physiol. 86: 1421-1427, 1999.

63.  West, J.B.: *Respiratory Physiology - the essentials,* 5th edition. Williams & Wilkins, Baltimore, MD, 1995.

# INDEX

# G

# H

## T - U - V - W - X - Y - Z